Focus ENGLISH

Teacher's

Anthology
4

Written and compiled by
Chris Buckton and **Pie Corbett**

Series Editor: **Leonie Bennett**

Heinemann

Heinemann Educational Publishers
Halley Court, Jordan Hill, Oxford OX2 8EJ
a division of Reed Educational & Professional Publishing Limited

Heinemann is a registered trademark of Reed Educational & Professional Publishing Limited

OXFORD
MELBOURNE AUCKLAND
IBADAN JOHANNESBURG GABORONE BLANTYRE
PORTSMOUTH NH (USA) CHICAGO

© Reed Educational and Professional Publishing 1999
First published 1999

03 02 01 00 99
10 9 8 7 6 5 4 3 2 1

British Library Cataloguing in Publication Data
A catalogue record for this book is available from the British Library.

ISBN 0 435 10691 0

Designed by Claire Brodmann Book Designs, Burton-on-Trent
Colour reproduction by Ambassador Litho, Bristol
Printed in Spain

Contents

Guide to using the Teacher's Anthology

Welcome to the *Teacher's Anthology*! This book is the core of **Focus English** and contains all the information you will need to run a Literacy Hour or English lesson. We strongly recommend that it is not stored centrally or in the staff-room. Each teacher will need a copy readily accessible. You will also need a copy of the *Teacher's File*, which contains background notes on the programme, together with termly tests and 33 photocopiable worksheets.

This book contains extracts, notes and suggestions for the 28 units of **Focus English** Year 4. For each unit, two main things are provided:

- literacy lesson pages, with teaching points and advice (to help you run the lesson)
- annotated extracts (for you to read with the class and answer questions)

Main learning objectives are stated at the head of each unit. They show the elements of the National Literacy Strategy Framework which the unit has been designed to teach. Additional work in the unit (for further Literacy Hours) covers other objectives. NLS references to all these objectives can be found in the *Teacher's File*.

If you wish to complete the main sections in one Literacy Hour, it's suggested you time the hour as follows

- read the extract and go through the questions   *20–30 minutes*
- guided reading; reading/writing activities   *20–30 minutes*
- plenary   *10 minutes*

There is enough work in the related activities for each unit to be used for a week's lessons. You may wish to spend longer exploring the questions and activities in greater depth, depending on the needs of the class. A glossary of terms can be found at the end of the book.

How do I run a lesson using the Teacher's Anthology?

First select the unit you wish to teach, using the contents page in the pupil's *Anthology* and the correlation charts in the *Teacher's File*.
In the Teacher's Anthology *turn to the relevant Literacy Lesson page for the unit.*

Whole class

1 Introduction

Read this introduction aloud to the class. It explains the context of the extract and introduces the learning objectives. You may wish to outline these to the class.

Move on to the annotated extract. (You will find the relevant page numbers at the end of the introduction.)

2 Annotated extract

Read the extract to the children. Discuss the questions at the end of the extract. You can use the prompts at the top of the page and around the text to help you guide the discussion. The questions help the children to understand the text and reinforce the learning objectives. They also lead in to the reading and writing activities.

Return to the relevant Literacy Lesson page. This will give you directions and support for all the following work.

3 Activities: Reading

Direct the children to the relevant page in their *Skills Books*. *Reading Skills Book A* may be used initially by most children in the class. *Reading Skills Book B* is aimed at higher attaining children. You can move children between Book A and Book B as you think appropriate. There will be considerable overlap, so that all pupils can take part in the plenary session. The relevant Worksheets can be found in the *Teacher's File*.

4 Guided Reading/Extension work

These are additional activities which can be led by you in a guided reading session whilst the rest of the class are working with the *Skills Books,* or be given to children who need a more demanding task or who finish early.

Whole class

5 Plenary discussion

Lead the class in a discussion to round up the lesson. The suggestions provided will help you draw the class together and talk about the work they have been doing independently.

6 Homework

If you wish, use these suggestions for related work to give the children as homework.

The tasks do not require any of the books to be taken home.

Additional activities

Sentence and word work

These are suggestions for whole class work at sentence or word level which relate to the extract. You can use these within the 'whole class' section for a full lesson, or you can use them for work which isn't directly connected to the shared text – e.g., to practise spelling high frequency words. They can also form the basis for another Literacy Hour.

Activities: Writing

This provides you with directions to the *Writing Skills Book* for a further Literacy Hour.

Written work for each unit starts with a shared activity which leads, step by step, towards a writing task (usually in the same genre as the shared text). This task may be carried out singly or in pairs. Here is a lesson plan for a Literacy Hour devoted to Writing Skills:

1 Introduction

Begin by introducing the extract again, using the prompts in the *Writing Skills Book.*

2 Shared Writing session

Use the suggestions in the *Writing Skills Book* to lead this session. You should demonstrate the writing process in full view of the class, on a board or on an enlarged photocopy of the relevant worksheet. Please see the *Teacher's File* (page 8) for further guidance.

3 Independent work

Use the suggestions provided in the *Writing Skills Book* to give the children a writing task. Differentiation will be by outcome: some children will tackle fewer questions than others; some will respond by writing a lot more. Suggestions in boxes show tasks that can be extended over time, or given to children who finish early.

Unit 1 : Mouldy's Orphan

Main learning objectives

- To investigate how settings and characters are built up from small details

- To use information about characters to predict their actions

- To link own experience to situations in historical stories

Whole class

Introduction

We are going to look at how we can find out about characters and settings from small details in a story.

This extract comes from a story set about a hundred years ago in Victorian times: 'Mouldy's Orphan' by Gillian Avery. It is about a labourer's family. Mouldy is a girl and is one of the children. Her mother and father have many mouths to feed, and life is very hard, but they do not think of themselves as being really poor. The really poor are the children without parents and without anywhere to live. If the really poor children are caught, they get sent to the workhouse. Mouldy finds an orphan, Benjy, who is living in the fields and having to beg for food. She brings Benjy home, but her family cannot afford to keep him.

Read the extract to the children and discuss it with them. Turn to pages 8–9 for the teacher's version of the text and Questions.

Independent work

Activities: Reading

- Reading Skills A (page 2) or B (page 2).
- The children working on Reading Skills A will need **Worksheet** 1 (Circle of Feelings: Benjy); those working on Reading Skills B will need **Worksheet 2** (Circle of Feelings: Benjy and Mouldy).
- To be worked on as an independent exercise.

Guided reading/Extension work

1 Read the first paragraph carefully. Why do you think the children 'held their hush'? *(Check that the children understand the phrase.)* What does it tell us about the character of Mouldy's dad?

2 How was Sunday different? What would Mouldy's mum be doing on the other days of the week? Discuss what the family might have eaten during the week.

3 Look at the small details of character revealed by, 'Billy didn't tease, nor May boss them all'. Why would Billy tease – what kind of things might he say and who would he tease? And why would May be the boss? Discuss the likely ages of the children.

4 Read the last paragraph. Why is Mouldy hysterical? Why does she repeat 'You can't, you can't'? Why does she think Benjy will die if he goes to the workhouse? How would she have said those words? Practise reading out her speech.

5 What is a 'furtive' look? Why do you think Benjy was furtive?
   (Furtive means secretive. He was expecting to get into trouble.)

Whole class

Plenary discussion

Ask pairs of children to tell the class which character they imagined they were, and what they would feel and do. Sum up the characters briefly in anticipation of the Shared Writing session later on.

Homework

Use **Worksheet 3** (Powerful Verbs), replacing 'ordinary' verbs with alternatives to add action and colour.

Additional activities

Sentence and word work

1 Spell two-syllable words containing double consonants: 'cottage', 'hammer', 'pudding', 'currant', 'struggle', 'suggest'. Look for other examples elsewhere.

2 Look at the spelling of 'shriek' and identify the phoneme. Collect different spelling patterns for the ee sound – 'receive', 'beak', 'feel'.

3 Identify powerful verbs: 'popped', 'stared', 'butted', 'flung', 'struggled', 'hammered'. Discuss their impact, or cover them for a Cloze procedure activity. Ask the children to suggest alternatives.

4 Adverbs: look at how they are used to show how the characters are speaking – e.g. 'savagely', 'hysterically', 'brightly'. Suggest adverbs to describe Flo's words (lines 23 and 30). Discuss the use of italics for emphasis in line 30.

Activities: Writing

● Writing Skills (page 4) – producing character sketches.

● Shared writing (teacher-led) is followed by an independent task.

The drawing activity (character sketches) is intended to check comprehension not to test drawing skill. It should be done with close reference to the text and to the notes made in Shared Writing. Make sure that the children spend no more than half the available time drawing.

Questions

1 How is Benjy different from the other children?
(He has different colouring, and doesn't know how to use a knife and fork.)

2 Why do you think Mouldy is drooping over her plate and not wanting any pudding? *(She's sad that they can't keep Benjy.)*

UNIT **1**

Mouldy's Orphan

Dad keeps strict order

clue that May's the eldest

Sunday dinner in Canal Row usually was a comfortable meal. The cottage had always been swept and polished the day before so there wasn't any cleaning, and even Mum took things more easily. Everybody felt peaceful. There was roast meat and gravy, and a pudding with currants in it, and with the children's father around they all held their hush; Billy didn't tease, nor May boss them all.

he seems so different

clue that she's the littlest

But today it was different. They were all quiet, certainly, but they were uneasy, looking at this stranger among
10 them. There had hardly been time to speak to Benjy, even if anybody knew what to say to him. They had squashed up to make room for him at the table, and Mouldy had Flo in her lap so that he could have her stool.

he's used to stealing and hiding food – expecting trouble

He looked so different from the others with their mouse-coloured hair and their rosy cheeks. Benjy had black hair and brown eyes and brown skin. He didn't seem to know how to use a knife and fork, but with furtive looks round the table, popped things into his mouth with his fingers. And Mum, who would never have allowed it in
20 the other children, let him be. They stared at him, all except Mouldy, who drooped over her plate. She didn't even want any pudding.

resentful

'That's our Billy's trousers he's wearing,' said Flo at last. 'Mum, our Mouldy's holding me that tight I can't breathe. Can't I get down? Is he going to stay here for ever and ever? Won't I never have my stool back?'

'I'm going along to see the Vicar this afternoon. While you're all at Sunday school. And you'd better run along now, quick sharp, or you'll be late.'

4

3 Why does Benjy give a shriek? *(He's frightened of the workhouse.)*

4 a) What do you think a workhouse is? *(Designed as places where the very poor could go for food and shelter, workhouses were made harsher than the worst conditions outside to put people off. Families were separated. Work was very hard.*

Punishments for misbehaving were harsh. The food was just enough to keep people alive.)

b) Do you think there are workhouses today? *(No, we've had a different welfare system since the 1920s.)*

30   'Is *he* coming with us?' said Flo.

'He's going to come to the Vicarage with me.'

'Will he be there when we come back then?'

'I don't know, and that's the end of it. So get your coats on, and Flo, you come here while I pin your scarf round you.'

'Perhaps they'll take him off to the workhouse.' suggested May brightly. 'That's where people get took as hasn't any homes.'

Up till then, Benjy had been quite quiet, accepting the 40 clothes they had put on him and the food that had been set before him. But now he gave a shriek and pushed his way towards the door. He couldn't get out. Billy was leaning his back against it as he struggled to lace up his boots, but Benjy hammered his fists on it.

'I'm not going to no work'us. I've run away all the time from those as wanted to take me there. What did you go bringing me here for?' he shouted savagely at Mouldy. 'You said you was taking me to a proper home where there was a baby. I didn't ask to come. You said come.'

50   Mouldy flung herself hysterically at her mother. 'You can't let him go to the workhouse.' She butted Mum's apron front. 'You can't, you can't. It's prison, that's what it is. I've seen the one in Brackley. He'll die if he goes there.'

Gillian Avery

fear of workhouse

strong verbs

adverbs adding colour to words of speakers

desperate emphasis

Questions

1 | How is Benjy different from the other children?
2 | Why do you think Mouldy is drooping over her plate and not wanting any pudding?
3 | Why does Benjy give a shriek?
4 | **a)** What do you think a workhouse is?
  | **b)** Do you think there are workhouses today?

5

Unit 2 : The Bully Asleep

Main learning objectives

- To read and understand a poem on a common theme, considering form and language

- To discuss personal responses and preferences

Whole class

Introduction

This poem is written by John Walsh. It is about a group of school children and their teacher, Miss Andrews.

Read the poem to the children and discuss it with them. Turn to pages 12–13 for the teacher's version of the text and Questions.

Independent work

Activities: Reading

- Reading Skills A (page 3) or B (page 3).
- To be worked on as an independent activity.

Guided reading/Extension work

1 Re-read the poem together. Discuss and list on a chart what the other children felt about Bill.

2 Discuss which is the most important verse in the poem.

3 List together the most important lines or words from the poem. For instance: 'timidly', 'his mother doesn't care', 'now's a good chance', 'so they plotted', 'Jane sat wide-eyed', 'their cruelty gone', 'tearful and foolish, wanted to comfort him', are all crucial to the poem.

4 Does the poet feel sorry for the children or for Bill? How does the poet feel about Jane?

5 What might Jane have written in her diary that night?

Whole class

Plenary discussion

Why did Jane feel foolish? Discuss with the children what they thought. Listen to their likes/dislikes about the poem. Encourage them to quote from the text. They may want to discuss memories, things the poem reminded them of, feelings, fears, actual words or phrases that sounded effective.

Homework

Use **Worksheet 4** (Edit a Poem). This is an example of the first draft of a poem. Your task is:

● to trim down some of the sentences and cut out words that are not needed.

Additional activities

Sentence and word work

1 Through a shared writing session, rewrite the poem, changing the verbs from the past to the present tense. Re-read both poems to see which sounds better – past or present tense. Remind the children that one way of testing if a word is a verb is to see whether the tense can be changed.

2 Re-read the poem and identify the main verbs. Try changing those verbs for others that could be used in their place. Decide which new verbs add to the meaning and sound effective.

3 Re-read the poem and insert adverbs beside the verbs. Does this add or detract from the impact?

Activities: Writing

● Writing Skills (page 6) – writing a short, 'angry words' poem, using similes.

● Shared writing (teacher-led) is followed by an independent task.

1 What is the name of the child who fell fast asleep? *(Ask the children to re-read the first verse – it is important that they get used to double checking the reading rather than relying on memory. He is called Bill Craddock.)*

2 Why do you think they 'lifted his head *timidly*'? *(Various reasons – but make sure they re-read the first five verses and look for clues. Possible responses include: they do not want to wake him; he might get cross because he is a bully; they feel sorry for him because of his mother; they know he must be tired because he stays up all night; they want to take the chance to fill his pockets with things.)*

alternate lines rhyme

UNIT 2

The Bully Asleep

three examples of alliteration

One afternoon, when grassy
Scents through the classroom crept,
Bill Craddock laid his head
Down on his desk, and slept.

The children came round him:
Jimmy, Roger, and Jane;
They lifted his head timidly
And let it sink again.

10 'Look, he's gone sound asleep, Miss,'
Said Jimmy Adair;
'He stays up all the night, you see;
His mother doesn't care.'

reasons for his sleeping/bullying

'Stand away from him, children.'
Miss Andrews stooped to see.
'Yes, he's asleep; go on
With your writing, and let him be.'

6

3 What reason does Jimmy Adair give for the boy's falling asleep (third verse)? *(He stays up all night; his mother does not care. Does she go out to work, or is it that she does not bother to make sure that he gets to bed on time?)*

4 Who felt sorry for him? *(The last two lines show that Jane did. Keep this discussion brief, as this is covered in the skills books.)*

'Now's a good chance!' whispered Jimmy;
And he <u>snatched</u> Bill's pen and hid it.
'Kick him under the desk, hard;
20 He won't know who did it.'

expressive verb

'Fill all his pockets with rubbish –
Paper, apple-cores, chalk.'
So they plotted, while Jane
Sat <u>wide-eyed</u> at their talk.

<u>Not</u> caring, <u>not</u> hearing,
<u>Bill Craddock he slept on;</u>
Lips parted, eyes closed –
Their cruelty gone.

repetition for effect

inversion

'Stick him with pins!' muttered Roger.
30 'Ink down his neck!' said Jim.
But Jane, tearful and foolish,
Wanted to comfort him.

John Walsh

Questions

1 What is the name of the child who fell fast asleep?
2 Why do you think they 'lifted his head *timidly*'?
3 What reason does Jimmy Adair give for the boy's falling asleep (third verse)?
4 Who felt sorry for him?

7

Unit 3 : Castle

Main learning objectives

- To identify a text type
- To select and examine an opening sentence that sets a context, picking out key sentences and phrases that convey information
- To identify the key features of an instructional text

Whole class

Introduction

This piece of writing is taken from a computer game manual. The game is an adventure in which you defend a castle against different enemies. While we are reading it through, think about what type of writing it is and try to spot any words that are typical of this kind of writing.

Read the game to the children and discuss it with them. Turn to pages 16–17 for the teacher's version of the text and Questions.

Independent work

Activities: Reading

- Reading Skills A (page 4) or B (page 4).
- To be worked on as an independent exercise.

Guided reading/Extension work

1 Re-read the section that tells you what to do. In each paragraph identify the reason for doing each thing.

2 Identify well chosen verbs. Try adding an adverb. Does this improve the text? Encourage the children to use the correct terminology.

Whole class

Plenary discussion

Work out with the class the basic structure of a piece of instructional writing. Create a chart by asking the children what the first paragraph tells the reader *(what the instructions are about/why they are needed)*, then the next three parts *(what you need/materials; what to do, in order; and an end statement)*.

With the children list other instructions that they have read – for games, recipes, etc.

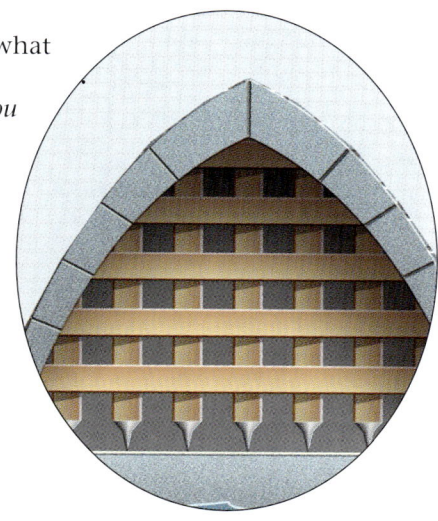

Homework

Use **Worksheet 5** (Defending a Tree-home). Ask the children to think of an imaginary creature who might live in it, and how that creature might defend itself against dangerous creatures such as dragons, goblins, spiders, wolves, eagles, dwarves and mischievous elves. They should sketch their ideas onto the worksheet; then label them carefully. The completed worksheet should be used in the Writing Skills section, where they are asked to write a set of instructions.

Additional activities

Sentence and word work

1 Point out the use of the **colon** and **bullet points**. Demonstrate how to use them when you are making a list of what you need – do this by swiftly listing what you need to play a well-known game, e.g. To play noughts and crosses you will need: 2 players, paper, 2 pencils, etc.

2 Look at the verbs in the extract. Where are they? *(Usually near the start of the sentences.)* Point out that they are **commands** – they tell you what to do 'fill, put, place, plant, smear, heat', etc.

3 List the words often used in instructions, such as 'first, secondly, next, after that, then, next', etc. Point out that these words can be left out if you use numbers to put the instructions in a sequence.

Activities: Writing

● Writing Skills (page 8) – writing a set of imaginative instructions for defending a hobbit's tree-home against enemies.

● This task accompanies **Worksheet 5** (Defending a Tree-home) for homework. The homework (a labelled drawing) should be done before writing the instructions.

Questions

1 What type of writing is this?
a diary
a description of an event
instructions
an advertisement

How do you know? *(Most children will spot that these are instructions. The clues are: opening statement; list of what you need; sequence of what to do, in order; words like 'first, second, then, after this' and 'finally'.)*

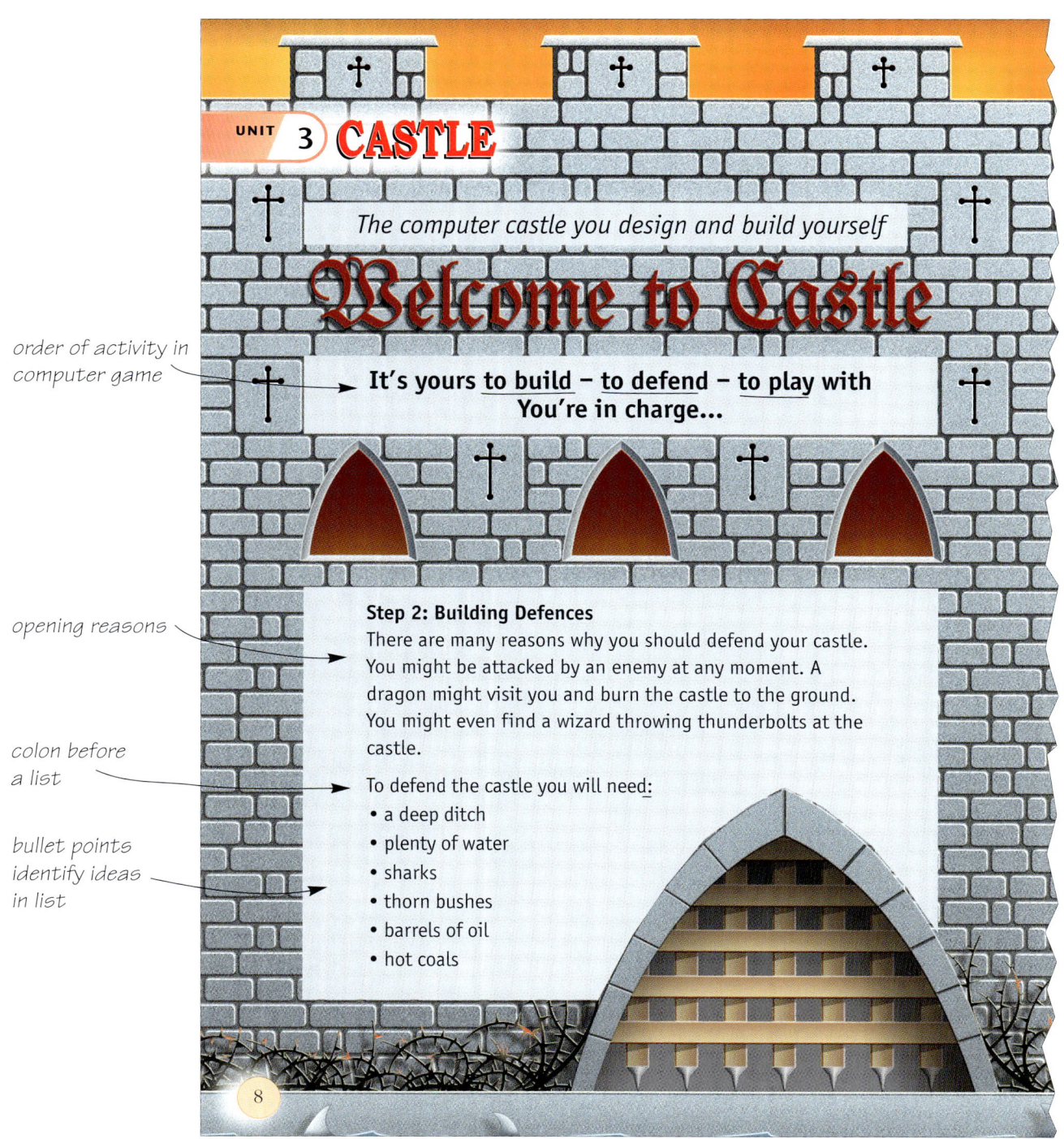

UNIT **3** **CASTLE**

The computer castle you design and build yourself

Welcome to Castle

order of activity in computer game

**It's yours to build – to defend – to play with
You're in charge...**

opening reasons

Step 2: Building Defences
There are many reasons why you should defend your castle. You might be attacked by an enemy at any moment. A dragon might visit you and burn the castle to the ground. You might even find a wizard throwing thunderbolts at the castle.

colon before a list

To defend the castle you will need:

bullet points identify ideas in list

- a deep ditch
- plenty of water
- sharks
- thorn bushes
- barrels of oil
- hot coals

8

2 What does the opening paragraph of step 2 tell you? *(It tells you why you need to defend the castle, it introduces the instructions, it explains what the instructions are about.)*

3 Which part of the extract might apply to a real castle? *(Various parts: dig a deep ditch; fill ditch with water; plant thorn bushes; heat up coals, etc.)*

4 Which part of the extract might apply to an imaginary castle? *(Sharks, thorn bushes that no-one can get through and smearing the walls.)*

5 Step 1 is missing. What do you think it might contain? *(Ask the children to read the opening heading and sentence – this suggests that the first step is to build the castle.)*

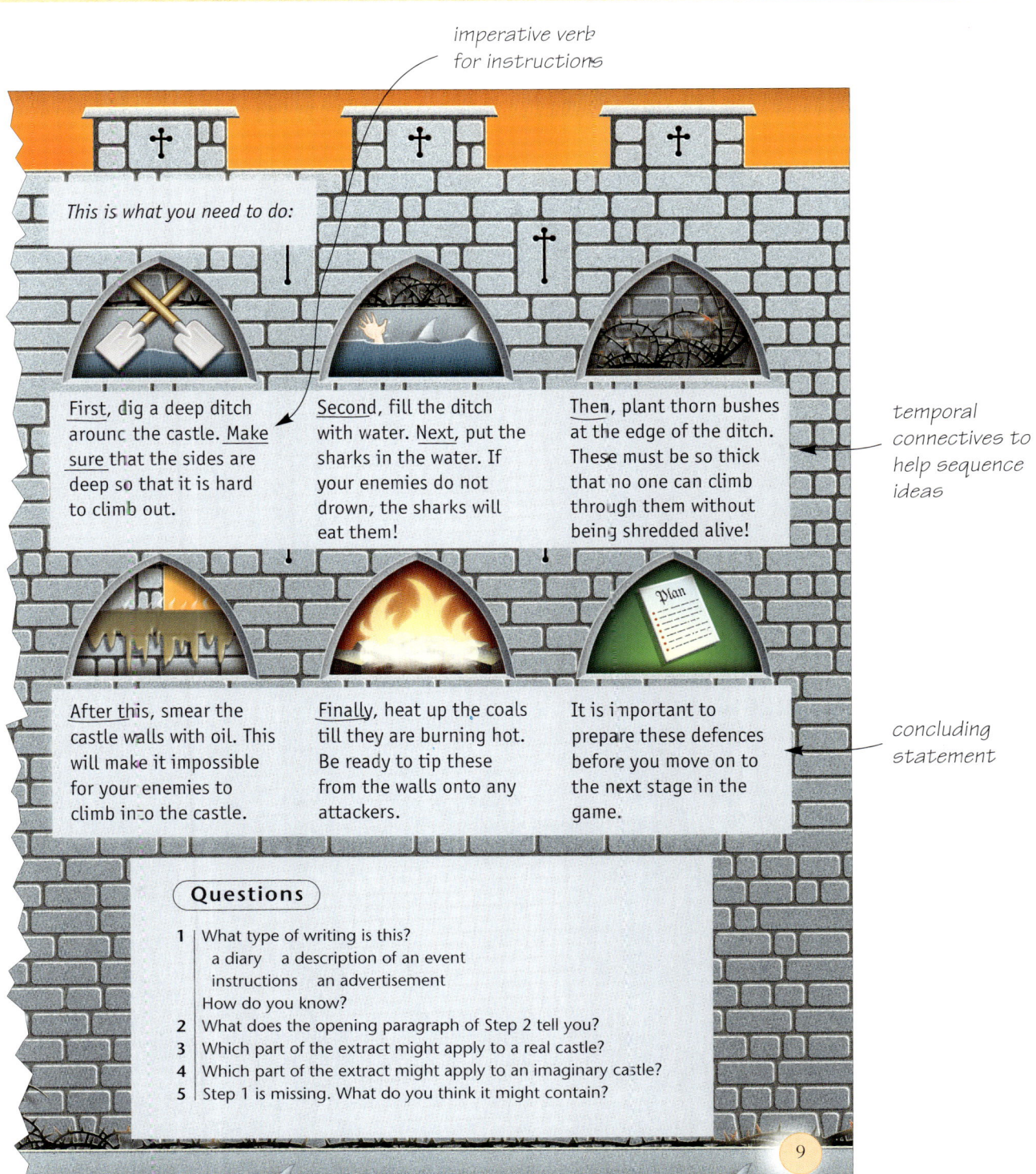

imperative verb for instructions

This is what you need to do:

First, dig a deep ditch around the castle. Make sure that the sides are deep so that it is hard to climb out.

Second, fill the ditch with water. Next, put the sharks in the water. If your enemies do not drown, the sharks will eat them!

Then, plant thorn bushes at the edge of the ditch. These must be so thick that no one can climb through them without being shredded alive!

temporal connectives to help sequence ideas

After this, smear the castle walls with oil. This will make it impossible for your enemies to climb into the castle.

Finally, heat up the coals till they are burning hot. Be ready to tip these from the walls onto any attackers.

It is important to prepare these defences before you move on to the next stage in the game.

concluding statement

Questions

1 | What type of writing is this?
    a diary   a description of an event
    instructions   an advertisement
    How do you know?
2 | What does the opening paragraph of Step 2 tell you?
3 | Which part of the extract might apply to a real castle?
4 | Which part of the extract might apply to an imaginary castle?
5 | Step 1 is missing. What do you think it might contain?

9

Unit 4 : Baboushka 1

Main learning objectives

- To compare organization of scripts with stories
- To identify main characteristics of key characters

Whole class

Introduction

The story of Baboushka is an old Russian legend. Baboushka lives in a little cottage in the middle of a dark forest. She is very house-proud, always busy, washing and cleaning and polishing. Then, one snowy night, there is a knock on her door. . .

Many different writers have told this story, and it has been made into a play as well. We are going to read part of it, from a book of myths and legends of the world, and then we are going to read the same part of the story, written as a playscript. We are going to spot the differences. We are also going to think about Baboushka's character.

Read the extracts to the children and discuss them. Turn to pages 20–21 and 22–3 for the teacher's version of the text and Questions.

Independent work

Activities: Reading

- Reading Skills A (page 5) or B (page 5).
- The children working on Reading Skills A will need **Worksheet 6** (Character Chart); those working on Reading Skills B will need **Worksheet 7** (Spot the Difference).
- To be worked on as an independent exercise.

Guided reading/Extension work

1   'Someone like me'. What does Baboushka mean? What kind of person is she? Do the children know anyone who is busy all the time, too busy to stop? What do they feel about Baboushka? Are they sympathetic or not?

2   What is the traveller called in the play? How could you show the audience who you were if you were acting the part? Why do you think there isn't a camel in the play?

Plenary discussion

Canvas the children's views about Baboushka. Will she be sorry if she doesn't go? What do you think will happen? *(This helps to anticipate the next unit as well as returning to one of this unit's objectives.)*

Homework

Use **Worksheet 8** (Busy Baboushka) to look at -ing words. This follows on from Sentence and word work.

Write scene 2 or scene 3 from the play (see Writing Skills Book).

Additional activities

Sentence and word work

1 Look at the **alliteration**, for example 'washing – wiping' (lines 40–42). Check that the children can use this term (introduced in *Year 3*, *Term 3*) and can give some more examples. Ask them to think of other verbs beginning with w, s, d.

2 Look at the spelling of -ing verbs: 'washing', 'wiping', 'sweeping', 'shopping'. Ask the children to try to work out the spelling rules, e.g. dropping the final e, 'wipe – wiping'; doubling the final consonant, 'shop – shopping'. Find more examples.

3 Cloze procedure: Cover the verbs in lines 7–12 and discuss alternatives.

Activities: Writing

● Writing Skills (page 10) – writing a playscript.
● Shared Writing (teacher-led), is followed by an independent task.

1 Who are Baboushka's visitors? What clues can you find? *(The Three Kings – rich clothes, camels, following a star, and their names.)*

2 What kind of person is Baboushka? What tells you this? *(Quite bossy – house-proud – she tells the visitors to wipe their feet even though she is feeling shy!)*

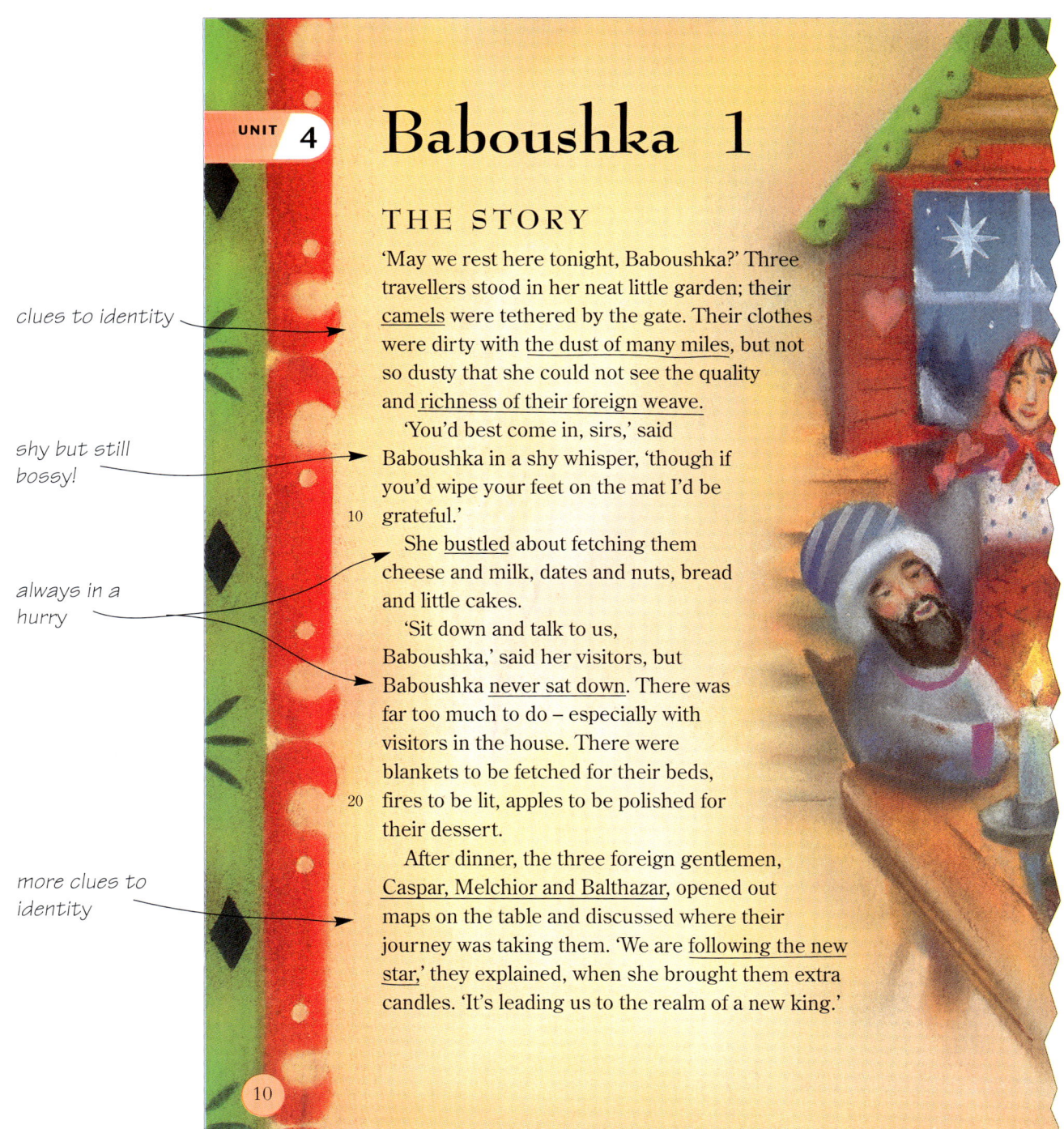

UNIT **4**

Baboushka 1

THE STORY

'May we rest here tonight, Baboushka?' Three travellers stood in her neat little garden; their camels were tethered by the gate. Their clothes were dirty with the dust of many miles, but not so dusty that she could not see the quality and richness of their foreign weave.

clues to identity

'You'd best come in, sirs,' said Baboushka in a shy whisper, 'though if you'd wipe your feet on the mat I'd be
10 grateful.'

shy but still bossy!

She bustled about fetching them cheese and milk, dates and nuts, bread and little cakes.

'Sit down and talk to us, Baboushka,' said her visitors, but Baboushka never sat down. There was far too much to do – especially with visitors in the house. There were blankets to be fetched for their beds,
20 fires to be lit, apples to be polished for their dessert.

always in a hurry

After dinner, the three foreign gentlemen, Caspar, Melchior and Balthazar, opened out maps on the table and discussed where their journey was taking them. 'We are following the new star,' they explained, when she brought them extra candles. 'It's leading us to the realm of a new king.'

more clues to identity

10

3 Where are the visitors going? Why doesn't Baboushka go too? *(To see the new king; she's too busy.)*

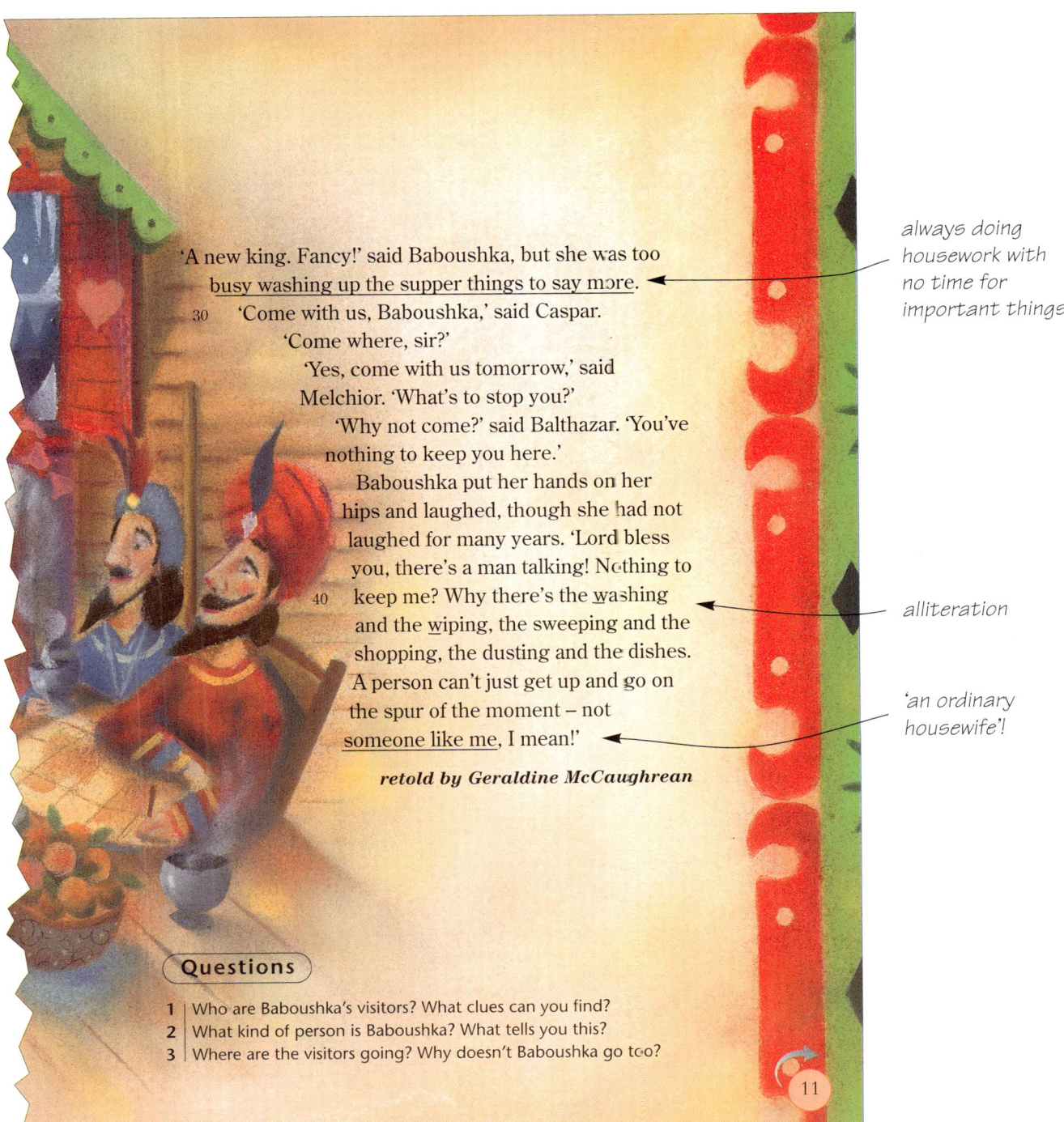

'A new king. Fancy!' said Baboushka, but she was too busy washing up the supper things to say more.

30 'Come with us, Baboushka,' said Caspar.

'Come where, sir?'

'Yes, come with us tomorrow,' said Melchior. 'What's to stop you?'

'Why not come?' said Balthazar. 'You've nothing to keep you here.'

Baboushka put her hands on her hips and laughed, though she had not laughed for many years. 'Lord bless you, there's a man talking! Nothing to

40 keep me? Why there's the washing and the wiping, the sweeping and the shopping, the dusting and the dishes. A person can't just get up and go on the spur of the moment – not someone like me, I mean!'

retold by Geraldine McCaughrean

always doing housework with no time for important things

alliteration

'an ordinary housewife'!

Questions

1 | Who are Baboushka's visitors? What clues can you find?
2 | What kind of person is Baboushka? What tells you this?
3 | Where are the visitors going? Why doesn't Baboushka go too?

11

4 How is the playscript different from the story? *(The way it is set out: only one king, no description, different details, e.g. food.)*

5 Why do you think there is no description of the king? *(Because you will see him on the stage.)*

name of character speaking in bold – no speech marks

stage directions in italic

only one King

anxious on her own

BABOUSHKA: THE PLAY

Baboushka has been giving a party for her friends. One by one they leave. Slowly she clears the table, looking out of the window from time to time.

Baboushka It's still snowing. I feel lonely now my friends have gone.

She sighs and sits by the dying fire holding her hands to the last of the heat. The First King appears outside the cottage. He looks tired and cold.

First King At last, a light! Perhaps someone will give me shelter.

When he reaches the door, he knocks. Baboushka looks out of the window. Then she opens the door just a crack.

Baboushka Who is knocking at my door so late at night?

First King Good evening, my lady. Do not be afraid. I have travelled from lands far beyond the forest. Please may I rest? I am very weary.

12

Baboushka Good evening, sir. Please come in. Why have you travelled so far on such a cold night? *The king enters.*

First King Have you seen how bright the stars are tonight?

Baboushka Yes, everyone is talking about it.

First King My wise men have told me to follow the brightest star of all. They tell me it will lead to the new baby king. Will you come with me, my lady?

Baboushka It is kind of you to ask, sir, but I can't. I have had <u>friends in all evening</u> so I must tidy my house. Will you have a cake and a glass of <u>wine</u> before you go, sir? *She passes him some cake and a glass of wine. He eats.*

First King Thank you for your kindness, my lady. Now I must be on my way. Farewell! *He goes out.*

adapted by Moira Andrew

compare with excuse in prose version

compare with food in prose version

(**More questions**)

4 | How is the playscript different from the story?
5 | Why do you think there is no description of the king?

13

Unit 5 : Baboushka 2

Main learning objective

● To chart the build-up of a play scene – opening and ending

Whole class

Introduction

Today we are going to read some more extracts from the play about Baboushka.

Recap the plot – Baboushka lives in a Russian forest – she is very houseproud, always working – the three kings call on her and ask her to go with them to follow the star but she is too busy. . .

In a story the writer can tell you all about the setting and the characters at the beginning. How can the playwright set the scene so that we know what it is going to be about? How do you think this play might begin?

Hold a brief discussion of any ideas – e.g. use a narrator, scenery, programme; show Baboushka cleaning her cottage and talking to herself; whatever the children suggest.

We are going to read the first page of the play.

Read the play to the children and discuss it with them. Turn to pages 26–7 for the teacher's version of the text and Questions.

Independent work

Activities: Reading

● Reading Skills A (page 6) or B (page 6).
● To be worked on as an independent exercise.

Guided reading/Extension work

1 Explore the children's different mental pictures of the setting: 'deep in the heart of old Russia', (and what does that phrase mean?), 'dark forest', 'winter's night', 'cottage'. What do they see in their mind's eye? Do different people have different pictures? Why do they think this is?

2 Look at the last speech. Why is it a 'forlorn' hope? Is Baboushka sad or happy at the end? How would you mime 'arriving at the empty stable, sadly leaving her gift'?

3 Why do you think the writer chose to have a choir singing a carol at the end of the play? What kind of atmosphere would it give? Do the children know the words? If possible, read them together.

Whole class

Plenary discussion

Explore the children's feelings about the end. How does the writer make it a mixture of sadness and happiness? Reinforce the point that we find things out in different ways in a play – through the narrator, the characters' words and the characters' actions. Make the link to the children's own writing.

Homework

Carry on writing the play of 'Little Red Riding Hood', remembering the three different ways of telling the audience – using a narrator, characters' words, and characters' actions.

Additional activities

Sentence and word work

1 Ask children to define some of the vocabulary in their own words: 'cottage', 'forest', 'pure', 'gift'.

2 Look at the use of the **present tense**: the play is happening now, in front of us. Compare it with the **past tense**: the story extract in Unit 4 is in the past tense. Practise changing tense.

3 Look at the use of adverbs to describe Baboushka's actions: 'sings *softly*', '*sadly* leaving'. Look at the different position of the adverb and how extra emphasis is added when the adverb comes before the verb. Try adding adverbs as stage directions, as preparation for independent work. Remind the children that adverbs generally end in -ly; and that they answer the question 'how' – e.g. How does she sing? She sings *softly*.

Activities: Writing

● Writing Skills (page 12) – writing a continuation of the playscript.

● Shared writing (teacher-led) is followed by an independent task.

Questions

1 What do we learn from this page? *(The characters in the play and the setting.)*

2 Why is there a storyteller (narrator)? *(So that the audience will know what's going on.)*

3 What do the words in *italics* tell us? *(Stage directions, sometimes put in brackets.)* Now we are going to look at how the play ends.

name of character speaking in bold – no speech marks

description of setting to help audience imagine the scene

clue to her hard-working character

stage directions in italics

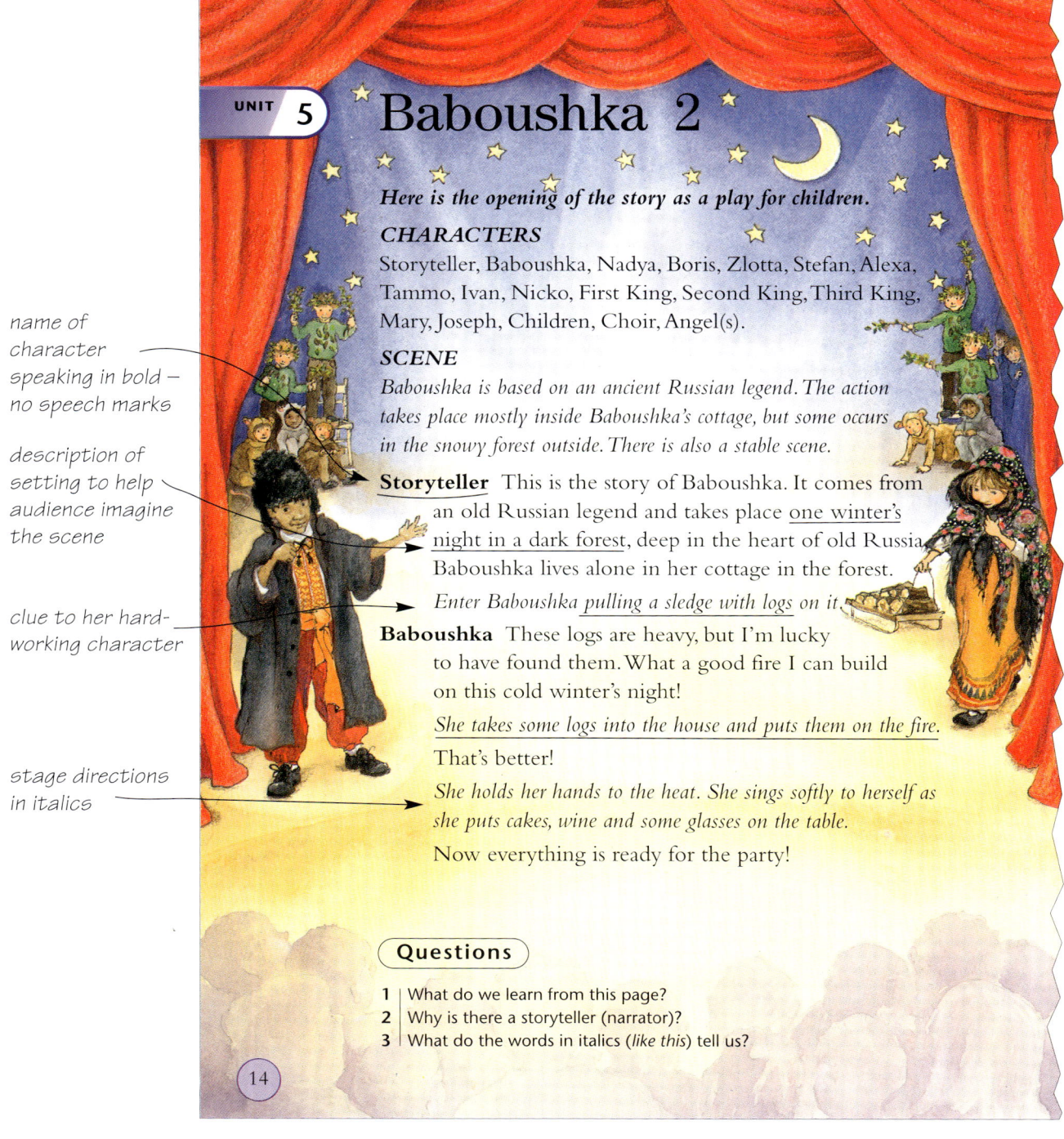

UNIT **5**

Baboushka 2

Here is the opening of the story as a play for children.

CHARACTERS

Storyteller, Baboushka, Nadya, Boris, Zlotta, Stefan, Alexa, Tammo, Ivan, Nicko, First King, Second King, Third King, Mary, Joseph, Children, Choir, Angel(s).

SCENE

Baboushka is based on an ancient Russian legend. The action takes place mostly inside Baboushka's cottage, but some occurs in the snowy forest outside. There is also a stable scene.

Storyteller This is the story of Baboushka. It comes from an old Russian legend and takes place one winter's night in a dark forest, deep in the heart of old Russia. Baboushka lives alone in her cottage in the forest.

Enter Baboushka pulling a sledge with logs on it.

Baboushka These logs are heavy, but I'm lucky to have found them. What a good fire I can build on this cold winter's night!

She takes some logs into the house and puts them on the fire. That's better!

She holds her hands to the heat. She sings softly to herself as she puts cakes, wine and some glasses on the table. Now everything is ready for the party!

Questions

1 | What do we learn from this page?
2 | Why is there a storyteller (narrator)?
3 | What do the words in italics (*like this*) tell us?

14

4 What does Baboushka do each Christmas? Why? *(She gives presents to all the children because she is still looking for the baby.)*

5 Does 'Baboushka' remind you of any other stories? *(St Nicholas, etc.)*

6 Do you think Baboushka is sorry that she did not go with the three kings? What makes you think that? *(She has been crying, she says 'I hope I'm not too late,' she sadly leaves her gift.)*

7 How does the play show us what happens at the end? *(Miming the actions while the storyteller speaks.)*

role of narrator is often important in a play

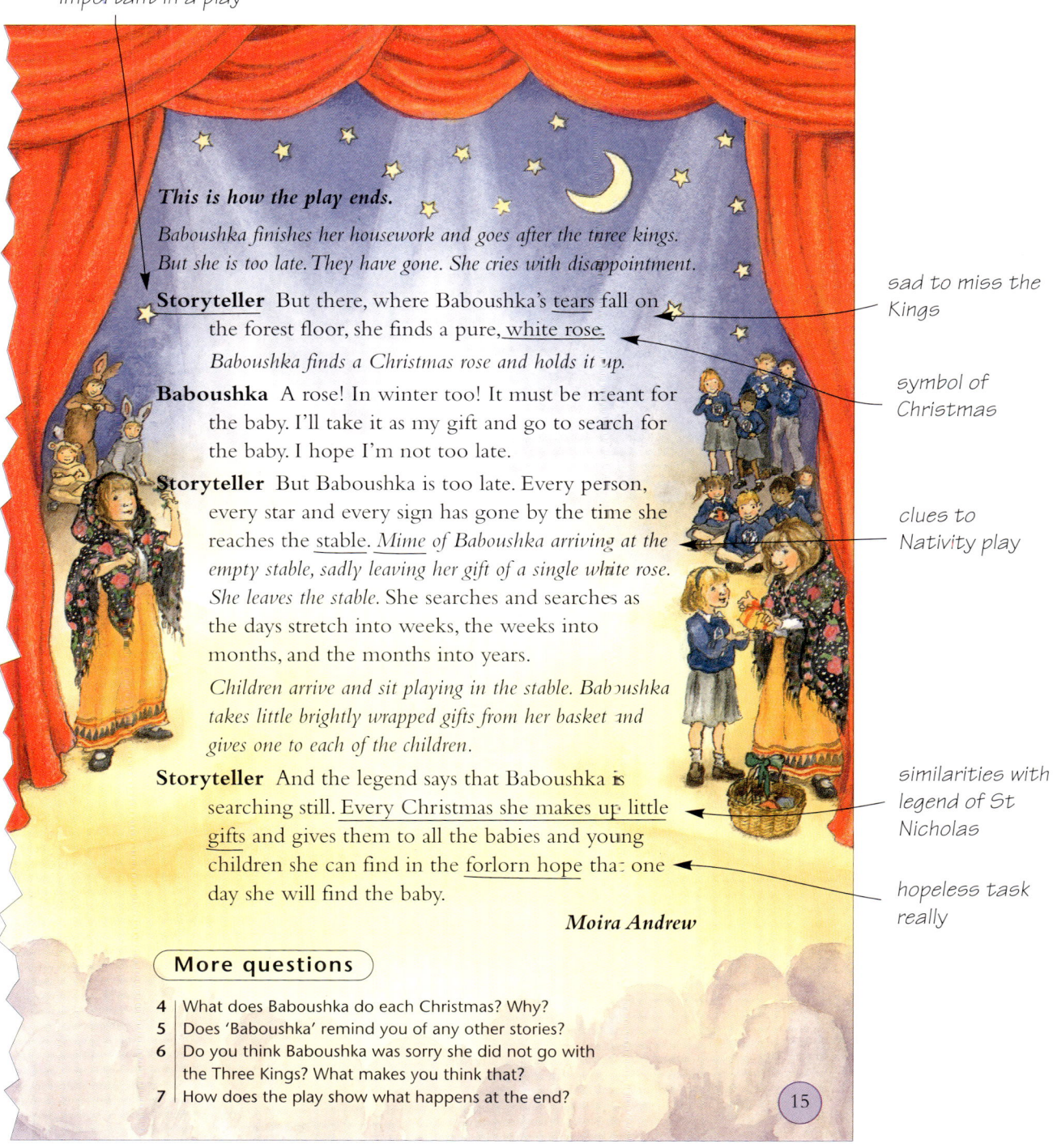

This is how the play ends.

Baboushka finishes her housework and goes after the three kings. But she is too late. They have gone. She cries with disappointment.

Storyteller But there, where Baboushka's tears fall on the forest floor, she finds a pure, white rose.

Baboushka finds a Christmas rose and holds it up.

Baboushka A rose! In winter too! It must be meant for the baby. I'll take it as my gift and go to search for the baby. I hope I'm not too late.

Storyteller But Baboushka is too late. Every person, every star and every sign has gone by the time she reaches the stable. *Mime of Baboushka arriving at the empty stable, sadly leaving her gift of a single white rose. She leaves the stable.* She searches and searches as the days stretch into weeks, the weeks into months, and the months into years.

Children arrive and sit playing in the stable. Baboushka takes little brightly wrapped gifts from her basket and gives one to each of the children.

Storyteller And the legend says that Baboushka is searching still. Every Christmas she makes up little gifts and gives them to all the babies and young children she can find in the forlorn hope that one day she will find the baby.

Moira Andrew

sad to miss the Kings

symbol of Christmas

clues to Nativity play

similarities with legend of St Nicholas

hopeless task really

More questions

4 | What does Baboushka do each Christmas? Why?
5 | Does 'Baboushka' remind you of any other stories?
6 | Do you think Baboushka was sorry she did not go with the Three Kings? What makes you think that?
7 | How does the play show what happens at the end?

15

Unit 6 : I Know Someone

Main learning objectives

- To read and respond to a poem on a common theme
- To discuss personal responses and justify preferences
- To discuss what makes a poem

Whole class

Introduction

This poem is by Michael Rosen, one of the most popular children's poets. He is a great performer of his own poetry. He writes about things that happen to his family and about his own childhood.

Read the poem to the children and discuss it with them. Turn to pages 30–31 for the teacher's version of the text and Questions.

Independent work

Activities: Reading

- Reading Skills A (page 7) or B (page 7).
- To be worked on as an independent exercise.

Guided reading/Extension work

1 Re-write a selection of the sentences as if they were part of a conversation, with two children boasting to each other, e.g. Tom stared at Sandy and muttered, 'Well I know someone who can take a mouthful of custard and blow it down their nose.'

   'That's disgusting,' said Sandy. 'Anyway, I know someone who can say the alphabet backwards.'

2 Discuss the title. What else could you call the poem? Can you think of a different title?

3 Take two of the sentences and turn them into newspaper headlines.

Whole class

Plenary discussion

Re-read this poem and 'The Bully Asleep' from Unit 2. Which do the children prefer? Divide the board in two and make a list of reasons for preferring one or the other poem.

Homework

Use **Worksheet 9** (Character Notebook) to make notes about people you know and what is special about them. You could write about friends, family, relatives, neighbours or even people in books or on television.

Sentence and word work

1 Read through each verse and list all the effective and powerful verbs. Try taking them out and changing them to see what effect it has.

2 Keep the verbs as they are and insert different adverbs to see if this improves the writing. If not, why is the poet's better?

3 Experiment by adding adjectives to see if this adds interest to the sentences.

4 Turn the statements into questions. How many ways can this be done? e.g.

Do you know someone who can. . ?

Who can. . ?

Is there anyone who might. . ?

Activities: Writing

● Writing Skills (page 14) – writing a poem like Michael Rosen's poem, full of strange and unusual boasts.

● Shared writing (teacher-led) is followed by an independent task.

Questions

1 Which is the most impossible boast? *(Various – a lot of children think the thumb idea is impossible – but there are some people who can do this!)*

2 Which one is the funniest? *(Various possible answers that can depend on how the poem is read.)*

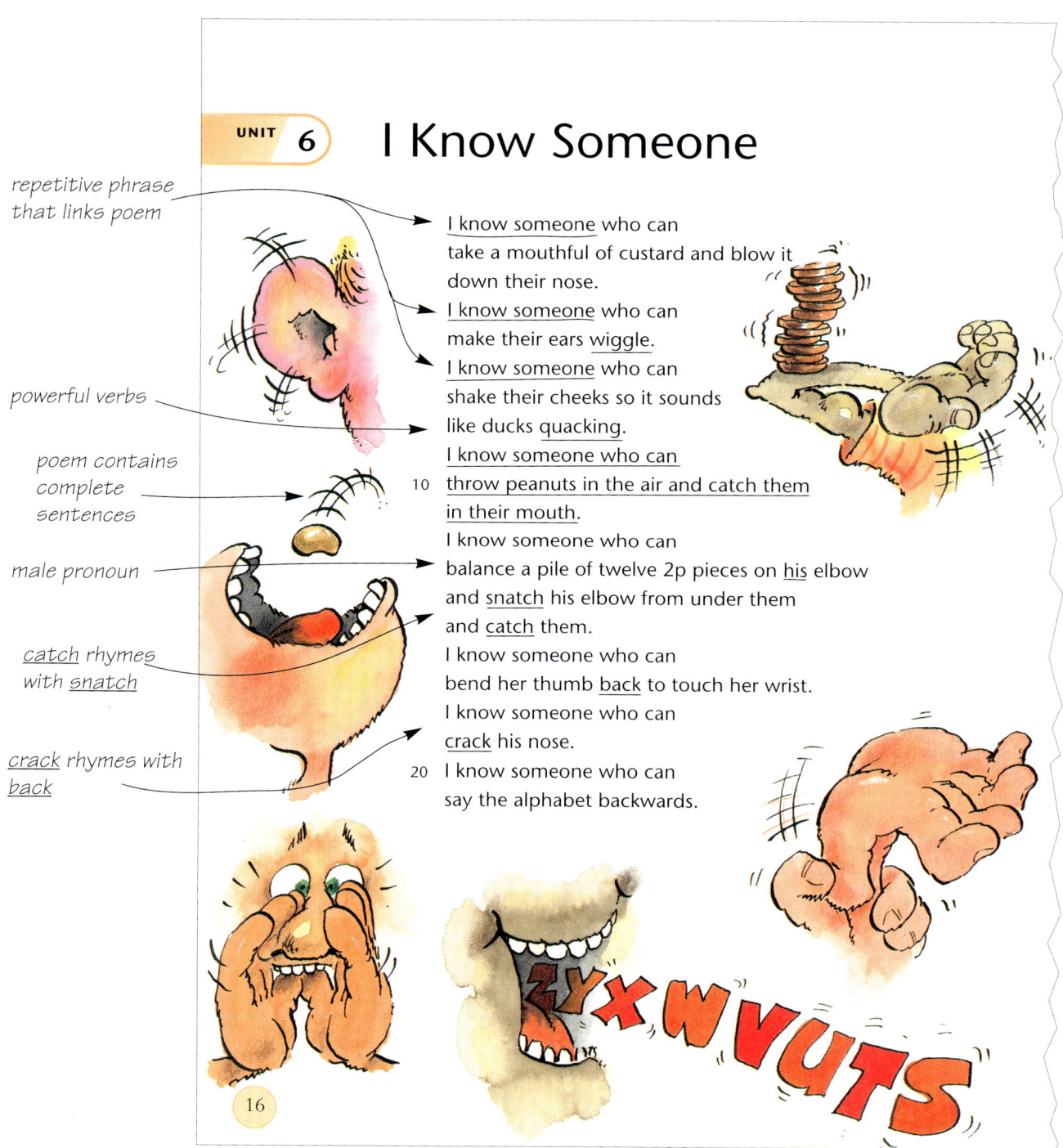

UNIT 6

I Know Someone

repetitive phrase that links poem

I know someone who can
take a mouthful of custard and blow it
down their nose.
I know someone who can
make their ears wiggle.

powerful verbs

I know someone who can
shake their cheeks so it sounds
like ducks quacking.

poem contains complete sentences

I know someone who can
10 throw peanuts in the air and catch them
in their mouth.

male pronoun

I know someone who can
balance a pile of twelve 2p pieces on his elbow
and snatch his elbow from under them
and catch them.

catch rhymes with snatch

I know someone who can
bend her thumb back to touch her wrist.
I know someone who can

crack rhymes with back

crack his nose.
20 I know someone who can
say the alphabet backwards.

16

3 **a)** Do you think this is a poem or a list of sentences? *(It is a list of sentences – and many children will happily describe it as a poem.)*

b) What makes you think that? *(It is not a story or a piece of non-fiction, so what is it? Some will say that it sounds more like a poem than anything else. Others may point out that the pattern on the page suggests that it is a poem.)*

4 Find three well-chosen verbs. (That is, verbs which give a good idea of the action which the poet wants to describe.) *(Focus on the first three 'verses' and identify – blow, wiggle, shake, quacking.)*

FPPPRRRRTTT!

I know someone who can put their hands in their armpits and blow raspberries.
I know someone who can
wiggle her little toe.
I know someone who can
lick the bottom of her chin.
I know someone who can
slide their top lip one way
30 and their bottom lip the other way,
and that someone is
ME.

Michael Rosen

female pronoun

capitals for emphasis

M E!

Questions

1 | Which is the most impossible boast?
2 | Which one is the funniest?
3 | **a)** Do you think this is a poem or a list of sentences?
   b) What makes you think that?
4 | Find three well-chosen verbs.

17

Unit 7 : Zoo Quest

Main learning objectives

- To identify different types of texts and their key features
- To examine opening sentences and key words or phrases
- To distinguish between fact and opinion

Whole class

Introduction

These two pieces of writing are about the same topic. But they are different types of writing. As we read them, think about what type of writing they might be and what clues you can find in the words.

Read both pieces of writing to the children and discuss them. Turn to pages 34–5 for the teacher's version of the texts and Questions.

Independent work

Activities: Reading

- Reading Skills A (page 8) or B (page 8).
- The children will need **Worksheet 10** (Who, Where, When?)
- To be worked on in pairs.

Guided reading/Extension work

1 Look carefully at passage **2**. Work out the structure of the writing together: (i) what is being discussed, (ii) reasons for/against, (iii) conclusion with reasons.

2 Draw the children's attention to the use of the colon and bullet points.

3 Find words or phrases that could be useful with any piece of writing which is written to persuade you, e.g. 'many people believe that', 'others think', 'reasons for/reasons against', 'I believe that', 'there should be'.

Whole class

Plenary discussion

Go over **Worksheet 10** (Who, Where, When?). Reinforce the structure of a recount: Who, Where, When, What and How did they feel?

Tease out the difference between the personal nature of passage **1** and the impersonal nature of passage **2**. In which passage do they feel they know the writer as a person? Discuss the purposes of the two types of writing.

Homework

Plan a poster to advertise a zoo. Include good reasons for visiting and supporting the zoo. Decide on the words you will use and sketch out the design.

Additional activities

Sentence and word work

1 Focus on the verbs in the recount (passage **1**). Make a list of them. Point out that when you write about what has already happened, you use the past tense.

2 Look at the spelling of words in the past tense. Think about how words often use -ed at the end. Focus on how a word like 'jumped' may sound like 'jumpt' but is a verb in the past tense and therefore has an -ed ending.

3 Change some of the verbs into the present tense with the children.

Activities: Writing

- Writing Skills (page 16) – writing a recount about a memorable event.

- Shared writing (teacher-led) is followed by an independent task.

1 **a)** What type of writing is passage **1**: instructions; poem; Description of an event (recount); story

   b) How do you know? *(Most children will recognize this as a piece of news. If they are unaware of the technical term introduce them to the word 'recount'.)*

2 What type of writing is passage **2**? How do you know? *(It is an argument, or discussion. Introduce the children to the term 'discussion' and 'persuasive writing'. We can tell it is a discussion because it gives reasons for and against.)*

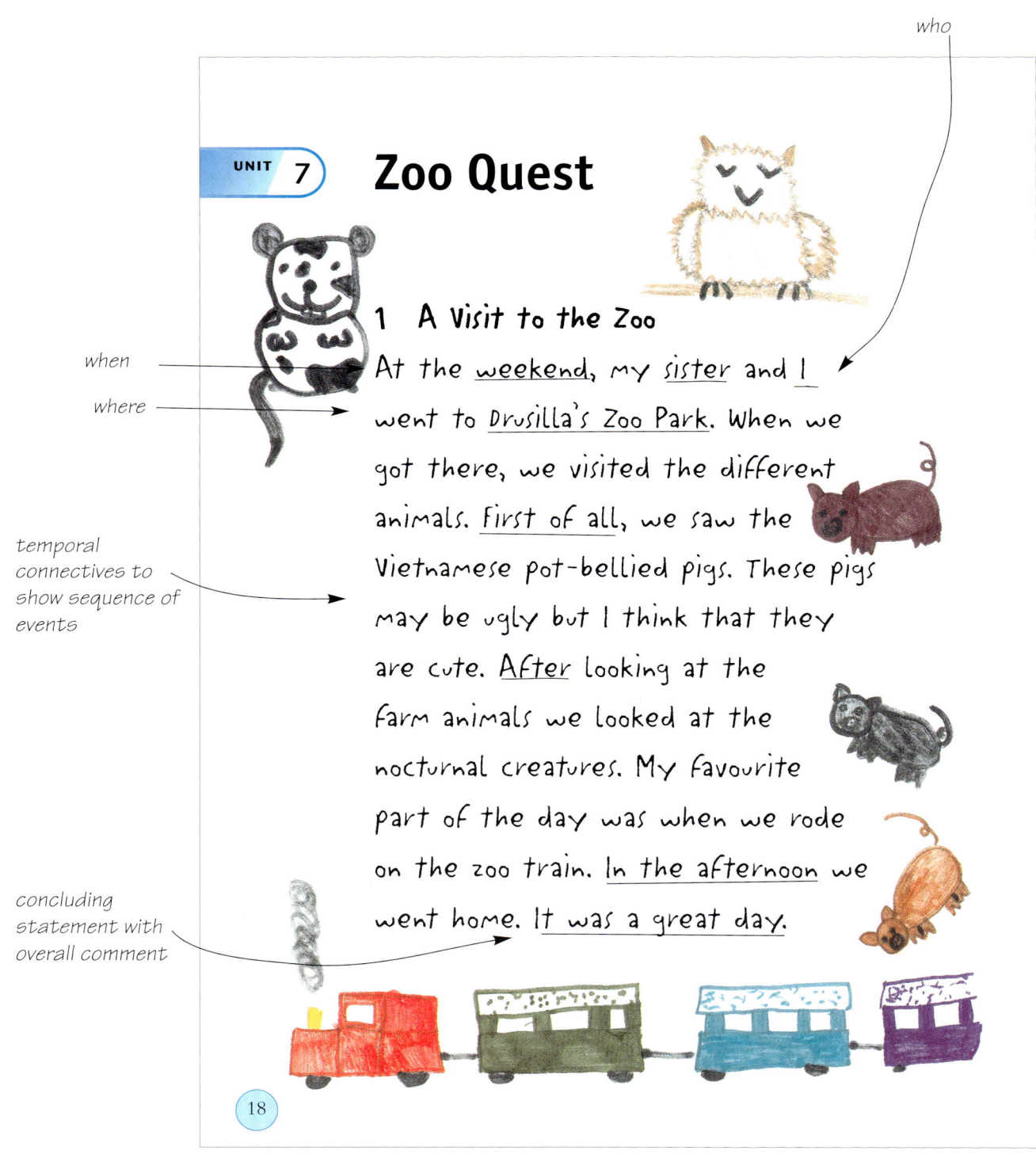

who

UNIT **7**

Zoo Quest

when

where

temporal connectives to show sequence of events

concluding statement with overall comment

1   A Visit to the Zoo

At the <u>weekend</u>, my <u>sister</u> and <u>I</u> went to <u>Drusilla's Zoo Park</u>. When we got there, we visited the different animals. <u>First of all</u>, we saw the Vietnamese pot-bellied pigs. These pigs may be ugly but I think that they are cute. <u>After</u> looking at the farm animals we looked at the nocturnal creatures. My favourite part of the day was when we rode on the zoo train. <u>In the afternoon</u> we went home. <u>It was a great day.</u>

18

3 In passage **1**, what information does the opening sentence give you? *(It tells you When (weekend), Who (my sister and I), Where (Drusilla's Zoo Park).)*

4 In passage **2**, what does the writer decide about zoos? *(Ask the children to look at the end of the piece. In persuasive writing, the writer usually sums up at the end. This writer decided that zoos do have an important job in education and in the preservation of rare animals.)*

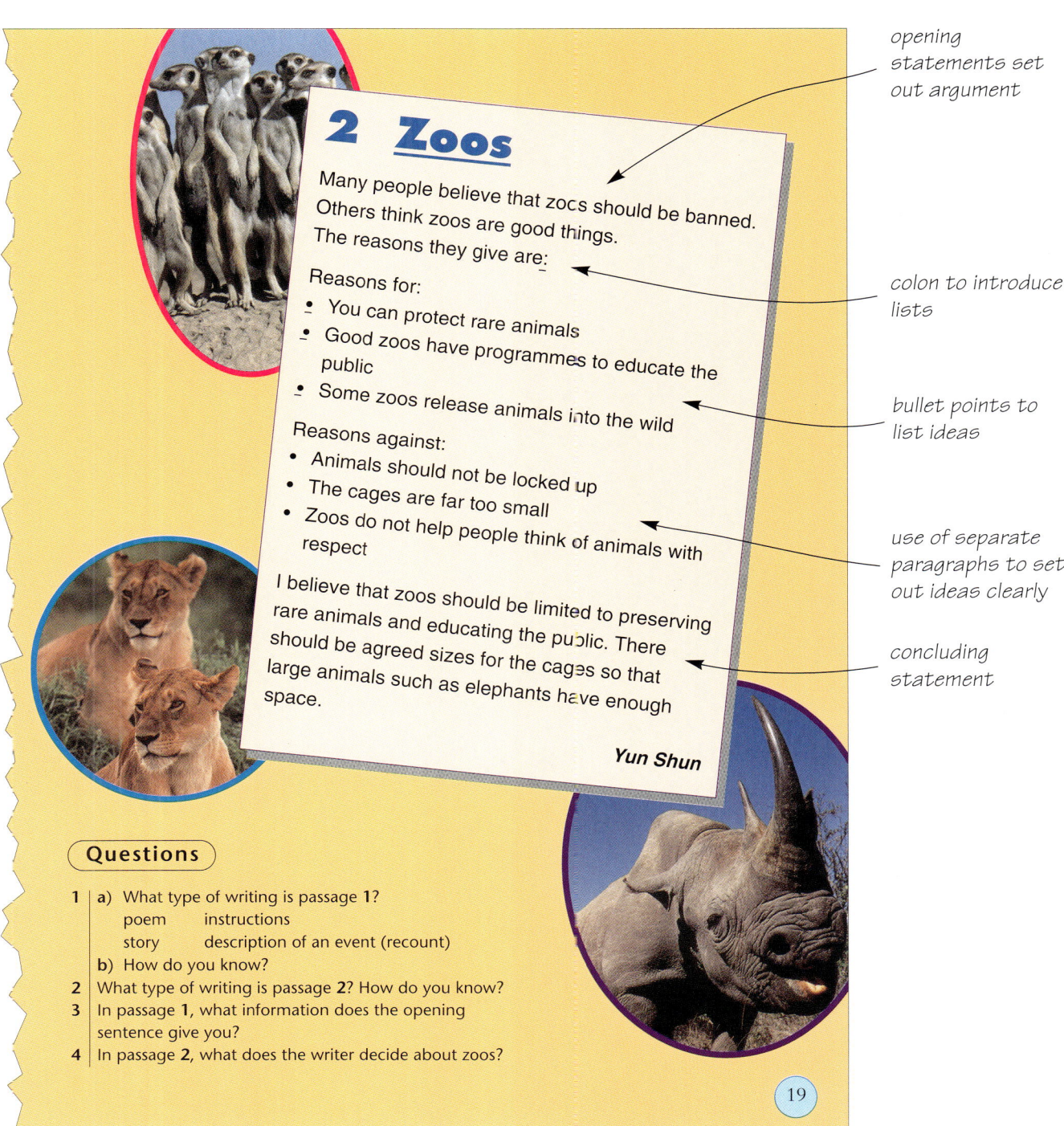

2 Zoos

Many people believe that zoos should be banned. Others think zoos are good things. The reasons they give are:

opening statements set out argument

Reasons for:

colon to introduce lists

- You can protect rare animals
- Good zoos have programmes to educate the public
- Some zoos release animals into the wild

bullet points to list ideas

Reasons against:

- Animals should not be locked up
- The cages are far too small
- Zoos do not help people think of animals with respect

use of separate paragraphs to set out ideas clearly

I believe that zoos should be limited to preserving rare animals and educating the public. There should be agreed sizes for the cages so that large animals such as elephants have enough space.

concluding statement

Yun Shun

Questions

1 **a)** What type of writing is passage **1**?
   poem   instructions
   story   description of an event (recount)
   b) How do you know?
2 What type of writing is passage **2**? How do you know?
3 In passage **1**, what information does the opening sentence give you?
4 In passage **2**, what does the writer decide about zoos?

19

Unit 8 : The Glass Cupboard 1

Main learning objectives

- To explore chronology in narrative
- To investigate how words and phrases can signal time sequences

Whole class

Introduction

'The Glass Cupboard' is a fairy tale with a moral at the end. Today, we are going to read the first part. We are going to think particularly about how much time passes in the story, and how the writer shows how much time has passed.

Read the first part of the fairy tale to the children and discuss it with them. Turn to pages 38–9 for the teacher's version of the text and Questions.

Independent work

Activities: Reading

- Reading Skills A (page 9) or B (page 9).
- The children will need **Worksheet 12** (Comic Strip).
- To be worked on as an independent exercise.

Guided reading/Extension work

1 Collect all the words or phrases connected with time: 'once', 'always,' 'whenever'. Brainstorm more words and phrases: 'First', 'After a while', 'Next', 'During the afternoon', 'By the evening'. Point out that these are more interesting than just repeating 'and then'.

2 Look at all the different ways in this extract of starting sentences. Use the opening as a model for the children to generate their own sentences: 'There was once' (a pink pig), 'Now, although' (he was only small he was very strong), 'For example,', 'If', 'Or'.

3 Look at the use of paragraphs in lines 29–50. When does the writer use new paragraphs? Try to work out some rules. (For example, time passing, change of subject, new person speaking.)

4 Explain that paragraphs are like boxes. The things in each box go together. You start a new box for something new – a new idea, or a new person speaking, or something happening in a new place, or a new time. Sometimes you start a new paragraph, because it is something very important and you want it to be in a box all by itself.

Plenary discussion

Introduce the idea of new **paragraphs** helping to show the order
things happen in – look at the paragraphs from line 17 'One of
the robbers. . .', 'Then the second robber. . .', 'Then the chief of
robbers. . .' Point out that many stories have this pattern.
(Three Bears, Three Billy Goats Gruff.)

Homework

This develops the Sentence and word work below.

Complete the punctuation question on **Worksheet 11** (The Lost
Punctuation).

Additional activities

Sentence and word work

1 Use of commas: (to prepare this, write out lines 6–11 on the
board, minus the commas and full stops). Discuss what commas
do – they make a pause, separate the different bits of a sentence,
help to make the meaning clear, mark off items in a list, etc.
Read lines 1–5 together, looking at where the commas are and
why. Then ask the children to shut their books and explain to
them that you have lost five commas and three full stops from
lines 6–11. Where should the pauses come? What clues tell you
where the full stops go? Then work out where the commas
could go. Do not insist on there being One Right Answer.

(Point out that the writer uses colons to introduce
dialogue, although you could use commas instead.)

2 Definitions: find alternative words or phrases for:
entirely   appeared   valuable   naturally

Then look up the words in a dictionary – explain that for
'appeared' you should look under 'appear'.

Activities: Writing

- Writing Skills (page 18) – writing an imaginative report.
  Children fill in a report form on **Worksheet 13** (Police Report).
- Shared writing (teacher-led) is followed by an independent task.

Questions

(1) What is special about the glass cupboard? *(You can take whatever you like out of it as long as you put something back in.)* What would you choose to take out?

(2) How long has the king owned the glass cupboard, do you think? *(Probably quite a while – everyone knows about it: 'you could always take out whatever you wanted'.)*

(3) Why can't the robbers sleep? *(They think they could be getting richer.)*

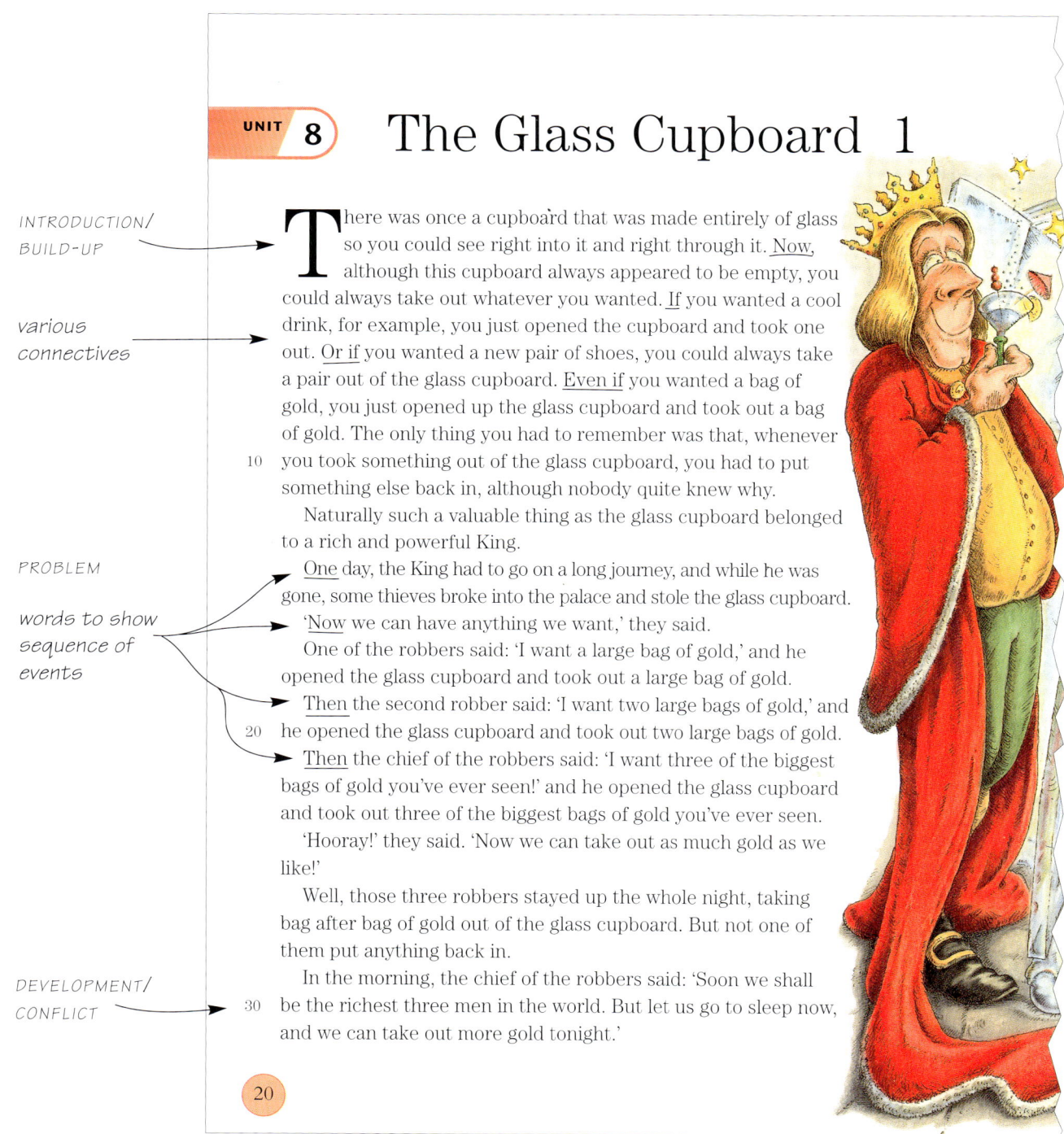

UNIT 8

The Glass Cupboard 1

INTRODUCTION/
BUILD-UP

various
connectives

PROBLEM

words to show
sequence of
events

DEVELOPMENT/
CONFLICT

There was once a cupboard that was made entirely of glass so you could see right into it and right through it. Now, although this cupboard always appeared to be empty, you could always take out whatever you wanted. If you wanted a cool drink, for example, you just opened the cupboard and took one out. Or if you wanted a new pair of shoes, you could always take a pair out of the glass cupboard. Even if you wanted a bag of gold, you just opened up the glass cupboard and took out a bag of gold. The only thing you had to remember was that, whenever

10 you took something out of the glass cupboard, you had to put something else back in, although nobody quite knew why.

Naturally such a valuable thing as the glass cupboard belonged to a rich and powerful King.

One day, the King had to go on a long journey, and while he was gone, some thieves broke into the palace and stole the glass cupboard.

'Now we can have anything we want,' they said.

One of the robbers said: 'I want a large bag of gold,' and he opened the glass cupboard and took out a large bag of gold.

Then the second robber said: 'I want two large bags of gold,' and

20 he opened the glass cupboard and took out two large bags of gold.

Then the chief of the robbers said: 'I want three of the biggest bags of gold you've ever seen!' and he opened the glass cupboard and took out three of the biggest bags of gold you've ever seen.

'Hooray!' they said. 'Now we can take out as much gold as we like!'

Well, those three robbers stayed up the whole night, taking bag after bag of gold out of the glass cupboard. But not one of them put anything back in.

In the morning, the chief of the robbers said: 'Soon we shall

30 be the richest three men in the world. But let us go to sleep now, and we can take out more gold tonight.'

20

4 Where does it tell you they took out lots of bags? *('bag after bag' lines 27–8, 'hard at it' line 56, 'more and more bags' lines 56–7)*

5 The third paragraph starts 'One day'. What other clues in the extract tell you time has passed? *('In the morning' line 30, 'So they lay down to sleep' line 33, 'so he got up' line 35, 'and then' line 36, 'meanwhile' line 33.)*

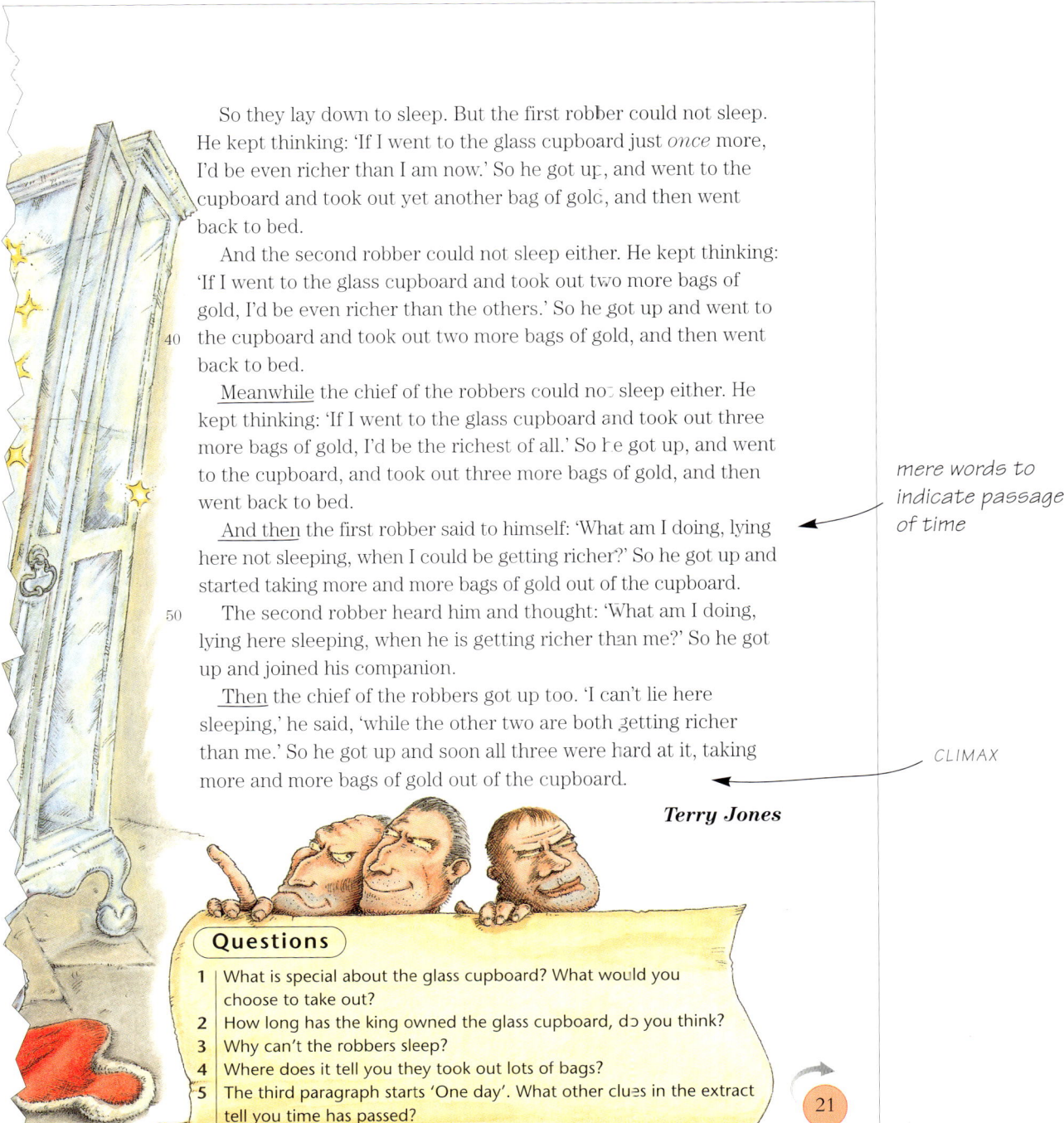

So they lay down to sleep. But the first robber could not sleep. He kept thinking: 'If I went to the glass cupboard just *once* more, I'd be even richer than I am now.' So he got up, and went to the cupboard and took out yet another bag of gold, and then went back to bed.

And the second robber could not sleep either. He kept thinking: 'If I went to the glass cupboard and took out two more bags of gold, I'd be even richer than the others.' So he got up and went to
40 the cupboard and took out two more bags of gold, and then went back to bed.

<u>Meanwhile</u> the chief of the robbers could not sleep either. He kept thinking: 'If I went to the glass cupboard and took out three more bags of gold, I'd be the richest of all.' So he got up, and went to the cupboard, and took out three more bags of gold, and then went back to bed.

<u>And then</u> the first robber said to himself: 'What am I doing, lying here not sleeping, when I could be getting richer?' So he got up and started taking more and more bags of gold out of the cupboard.

50 The second robber heard him and thought: 'What am I doing, lying here sleeping, when he is getting richer than me?' So he got up and joined his companion.

<u>Then</u> the chief of the robbers got up too. 'I can't lie here sleeping,' he said, 'while the other two are both getting richer than me.' So he got up and soon all three were hard at it, taking more and more bags of gold out of the cupboard.

mere words to indicate passage of time

CLIMAX

Terry Jones

Questions

1 What is special about the glass cupboard? What would you choose to take out?
2 How long has the king owned the glass cupboard, do you think?
3 Why can't the robbers sleep?
4 Where does it tell you they took out lots of bags?
5 The third paragraph starts 'One day'. What other clues in the extract tell you time has passed?

21

Unit 9 : The Glass Cupboard 2

Main learning objectives

- To explore chronology in narrative
- To explore narrative order: introductions/build-ups – climaxes or conflicts – resolutions

Whole class

Introduction

The children will need their comic strip stories (Worksheet 12) to refer to.

We are going to read the second part of the story about the Glass Cupboard. What has happened so far? Use **Worksheet 12** (Comic Strip) to remind you.

We are going to look at the different **stages** in the story. Most stories have stages something like this. I expect you know that a story needs to have a beginning, a middle, and an end.

Other words for the beginning are: **opening**, **build-up**, and **introduction**.

Other words for the stages in the middle are: **problem**, **complications**, and **climax**.

And the end is often called the **resolution**.

We will use some of these words today when we look at the stages in the story 'Glass Cupboard'. *(Write them on the board/wall.)* Do not worry if you cannot remember them straight away!

What happened at the very beginning of the story? *(The King went away on journey, robbers stole the cupboard.)*

The first part of the story was the build-up. Then there was the problem – the robbers wanted to take more gold than anyone else. Then there was the climax, which was the most exciting bit, when the robbers got more and more bags out of the cupboard. We stopped there. The next part of the story has a complication – because the robbers cannot stop! And then there is another climax before it is all sorted out at the end – the resolution.

Now read on. Turn to pages 42–3 for the teacher's version of the text and Questions.

Independent work

Activities: Reading

- Reading Skills A (page 10) or B (page 10).
- Children working on Reading Skills A will need to refer to their comic st0rip stories from **Worksheet 12**.

Guided reading/Extension work

Work with lower attainers

1 Go over the different stages of a story, this time using the story 'Little Red Riding Hood' as an illustration. Work out the stages

together, making notes as you do so. You could use **Worksheet 15** (Story Ladder).

Beginning (build-up): Red Riding Hood's mother asks her to go to her grandmother's.

Middle (problem, development): she meets the wolf and doesn't know his wicked plan.

Climax: The wolf eats her up.

End (resolution): The wolf is killed, the child is saved.

Then recap the stages in 'The Glass Cupboard'.

2 Look at the end of the story. Can you think of some of the things in the world that we use up, or take out of it? *(The children may think of oil, coal, trees, water. . .)*

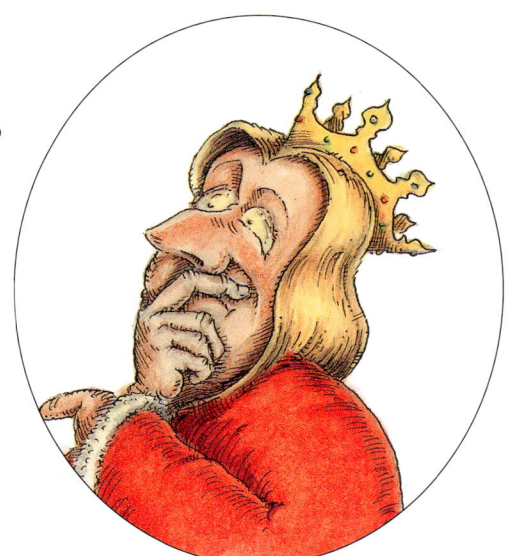

Whole class

Plenary discussion

Continue to add to the collection of 'time' words and phrases.

Ask the children to sum up how many days, weeks and months pass in the whole story, and ask them to show the clues in the text.

Homework

Change these verbs to the past tense. Use each one in a sentence.

return   throw   say   order   find   fill   take   hear   shake   put

Additional activities

Sentence and word work

1 Look again at the use of commas: the long sentence starting on line 66 is a good example. Ask the children to read the sentence aloud, showing the position of the commas with small pauses and careful phrasing. Try the last sentence as well.

2 Read lines 9–15. Look at the powerful verbs and phrases: 'could bear it no longer', 'smashed', 'gave a great cry', 'fell down dead'. Explore the effect of replacing them with something weaker: 'didn't like it any more', broke' ,'cried', 'died'.

3 Discuss more definitions: 'for fear that', 'at length', 'lack of sleep', 'kept at it' 'length and breadth of the land', 'fragile'.

Activities: Writing

● Writing Skills (page 20) – planning the stages in a story, using **Worksheet 14** (Story Plan). Followed by an independent task.

Questions

1 What is the **problem** for the robbers? *(None of them dares stop in case one of the others gets richer)*

2 What is the **conflict**? *(They are desperate with lack of sleep and food.)*

3 What is the **climax** in this part of the story? *(A robber smashes the cupboard and they all die.)*

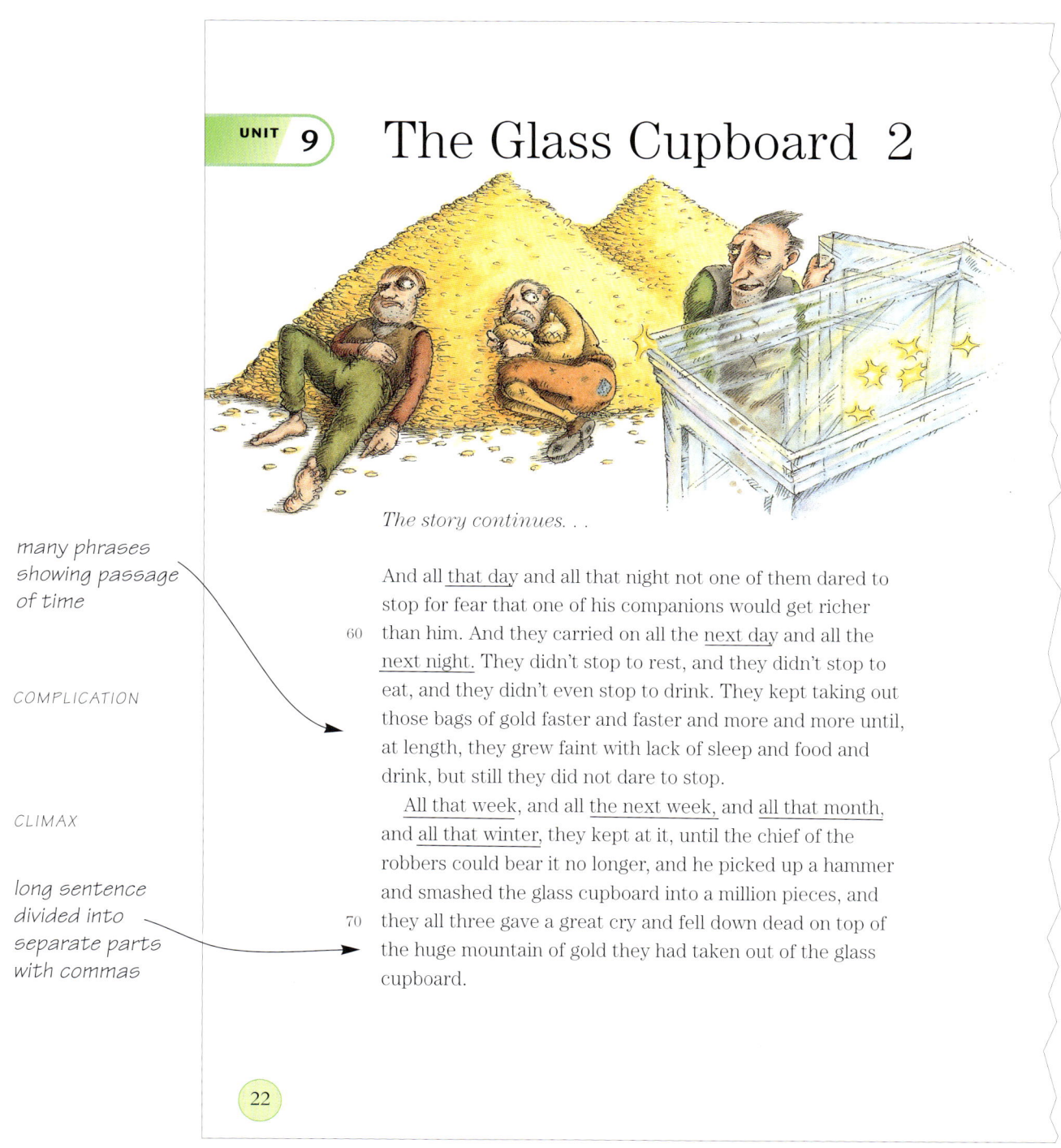

UNIT **9**

The Glass Cupboard 2

The story continues. . .

many phrases showing passage of time

COMPLICATION

CLIMAX

long sentence divided into separate parts with commas

And all <u>that day</u> and all that night not one of them dared to stop for fear that one of his companions would get richer
60 than him. And they carried on all the <u>next day</u> and all the <u>next night.</u> They didn't stop to rest, and they didn't stop to eat, and they didn't even stop to drink. They kept taking out those bags of gold faster and faster and more and more until, at length, they grew faint with lack of sleep and food and drink, but still they did not dare to stop.

    <u>All that week</u>, and all <u>the next week</u>, and <u>all that month</u>, and <u>all that winter</u>, they kept at it, until the chief of the robbers could bear it no longer, and he picked up a hammer and smashed the glass cupboard into a million pieces, and
70 they all three gave a great cry and fell down dead on top of the huge mountain of gold they had taken out of the glass cupboard.

22

4 How is the problem sorted out? (What is the **resolution**?) *(The King reminds everybody that the robbers forgot to put something back into the cupboard, and that is why they died.)*

5 Why does the King have the glass pieces melted down to make a globe? (This is the **moral** of the story.) *(The King wants to remind people that the world is like the cupboard – if we do not give back what we take out, the world will not survive. A moral is like a lesson.)*

Some time later, the King returned home, and his servants threw themselves on their knees before him, and said: 'Forgive us, Your Majesty, but three wicked robbers have stolen the glass cupboard!'

The King ordered his servants to search the length and breadth of the land. When they found what was left of the glass cupboard, and the three robbers lying dead, they filled
80 sixty green carts with all the gold and took it back to the King. And when the King heard that the glass cupboard was smashed into a million pieces and that the three thieves were dead, he shook his head and said: 'If those thieves had always put something back into the cupboard for every bag of gold they had taken out, they would be alive to this day.' And he ordered his servants to collect all the pieces of the glass cupboard and to melt them down and make them into a globe with all the countries of the world upon it, to remind himself, and others, that the earth is as fragile as that glass
90 cupboard.

new paragraphs are used to show the next event in the story

RESOLUTION

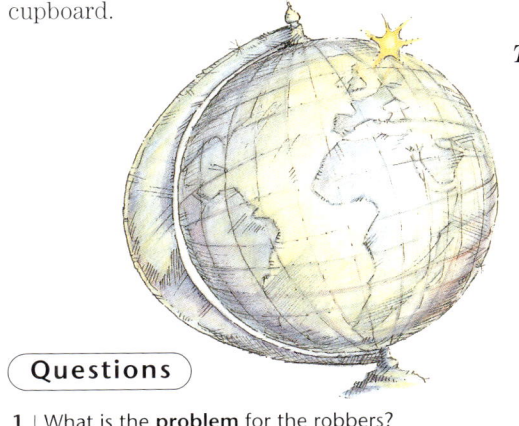

Terry Jones

Questions

1 | What is the **problem** for the robbers?
2 | What is the **conflict**?
3 | What is the **climax** in this part of the story?
4 | How is the problem sorted out? (What is the **resolution**?)
5 | Why does the King have the glass pieces melted down to make a globe? (This is the **moral** of the story.)

23

Unit 10 : School Bonanza!

Main learning objectives

- To understand and use the terms 'fact' and 'opinion'
- To identify typical features of a news item
- To predict newspaper stories from headlines

Whole class

Introduction

This is about a true event. Think about what sort of writing it is as we read it through. Which parts are facts and what is someone's opinion? First read the headline and try to guess what the writing might be about.

Read the newspaper story with the children and discuss it with them. Turn to pages 46–7 for the teacher's version of the text and Questions.

Independent work

Activities: Reading

- Reading Skills A (page 11) or B (page 11).
- To be worked on as an independent exercise.

Guided reading/Extension work

Work with lower attainers

1 Identify typical newspaper features in the layout and writing, e.g. headings, columns, photographs and captions, putting in ages, mixture of past and present tense, brief opinions from a few people, short paragraphs, not much description. How many adjectives are there?

2 **a)** Think up a different headline.

 b) Decide what the school will do with the money and then think up a headline for the follow-up story.

Whole class

Plenary discussion

Look at facts and opinions in the article. Discuss which typical features of a local newspaper article appear in 'School Bonanza'.

Homework

Use **Worksheet 16** (Lucky Lottery School). This is the first draft of an article for the local paper about what the school has done with the money. The journalist has been rather clumsy and careless.

1 Improve the writing.

2 Check for accuracy in spelling and punctuation.

3 Make any changes which will improve the way it is written.

The children could also collect some articles from local papers and bring them into school for a discussion of typical features.

Additional activities

Sentence and word work

1 Try to find the verb in each sentence. To check whether it is a verb or not, see whether it can be changed into the past tense. What happens if you take the verb out of the sentence?

2 Which are the key words in the first sentence?

3 Re-read the passage and show the children how to find the key words and phrases that a journalist might have used to make notes.

Activities: Writing

● Writing Skills (page 22) – writing a hundred-word newspaper account of a school event.

● Shared writing (teacher-led) is followed by an independent task.

1 What type of writing is this?
discussion/argument
newspaper report
story
diary
(Most children will recognize that it is a newspaper report.)

2 What clues tell you? *(Layout, typeface and style – some may be more specific, e.g. 'Sam, aged 7,' is what newspapers always write!)*

3 Find two facts. *(Ask the children to identify a real fact – e.g. the school has been left £250,000.)*

---

news headline →

summary of story in opening sentence →

basic details →

UNIT 10

SCHOOL

A small village school in the North Yorkshire moors has been left £250,000

Cumnor Primary School in Wissleton was left the money by Miss Evelyn Bradley in her will. She used to live in the village but had moved to London. In 1990, Miss Bradley sent a donation of £100 to the school. The children wrote back and have kept in touch ever since, sending news to her every year.

The school is in the village of Wissleton and has only 45 pupils.

24

4 Find two opinions. *(Parents would like a playground, Tiseme would like a tuck shop and Sam wants an adventure playground.)*

5 If this was your school, how would you spend the money? *(Various responses!)*

BONANZA!

short quote

The Headteacher, Mr Bruce Burn, said that Miss Bradley had <u>very fond memories of living in the village</u>. 'This came as a wonderful surprise.'

The school is not sure <u>what it will spend the money on</u>. Mr Burn said, 'Everybody has different ideas. At the moment we are asking the children and parents to let us know what they think.'

There is no playground, and parents have been concerned that their children have to play on the village green which is surrounded by three roads. The children have made various suggestions. Tiseme, aged 9, would like to see a tuck shop where you could buy chips at break-time. Sam, aged 7, thinks that the school needs an adventure playground.

different views and ideas

key issue in story

Questions

1 What type of writing is this?
   discussion/argument   newspaper report   story   diary
2 What clues tell you?
3 Find two facts.
4 Find two opinions.
5 If this was your school, how would you spend the money?

25

Unit 11 : Wish Wish Wish

Main learning objectives

- To read and understand a poem on a common theme
- To discuss personal responses and justify preferences

Whole class

Introduction

This poem is by Jackie Kay.

Read the poem through or ask several children to read the poem through in order to have a change of voice. They will need some time to prepare for this. Discuss the poem with them. Turn to pages 50–51 for the teacher's version of the text and Questions.

Independent work

Activities: Reading

- Reading Skills A (page 12) or B (page 12).
- To be worked on as an independent exercise.

Guided reading/Extension work

1 Discuss what the poet means by line 7. Does the poem reflect this line?
2 Discuss any advice that you could give this person.
3 In pairs, think of different rhymes. Alter the lines accordingly, e.g. line 7 could become, 'I wish my slippers were not pink'.
   (You could use a rhyming dictionary to help, if you have one.)

Whole class

Plenary discussion

Would the children like to have this person as a friend. Make two lists on the board – reasons for and reasons against. Make sure the children refer back to the text.

Homework

Use **Worksheet 17** (Missing Words), focusing upon selecting verbs.

Additional activities

Sentence and word work

1 Look at the verbs in the poem. Experiment by changing some of them. Write your new lines and compare them with the original. How is the effect different?

2 Add some adverbs. What effect does this have?. Use the terms verb and adverb.

Activities: Writing

● Writing Skills (page 24) – writing a wish poem.

● Shared writing (teacher-led) is followed by an independent task.

Questions

1. Do you share any of the poet's wishes? *(Various responses – the key thing is to ask the children to quote from the text.)*

2. Which wishes (if any) make you feel sorry for the writer? *(Various responses, again they must quote from the text. Some children may choose responses that relate to themselves as well as the writer – they know how she feels.)*

UNIT 11

Wish Wish Wish

repetitive phrase

I wish my mum didn't wear odd clothes.
I wish mine weren't secondhand.
I wish I didn't have such a big nose.
I wish I could escape to Neverland.

aa, bb rhyme pattern

I wish my eyes didn't constantly blink.
I wish I didn't wear glasses.
I wish I did something other than think.
I wish I looked like other lassies.

I wish my voice didn't shake.
10 I wish my hands wouldn't sweat.
I wish my life wasn't full of mistakes.
I wish I didn't always forget.

26

3 Are any of the wishes funny? *(Depending on the children's mood – and the way in which the poem is read – they may or may not have found the poem funny.)*

4 What patterns are there? *(Rhyming pattern – and the repetition of 'I wish'. The last words on the first and third lines, and the second and fourth lines, rhyme. Some words, such as 'clothes' and 'nose' are near rhymes – they share sounds but are not an exact rhyme.)*

I wish my freckles would move down my back.
I wish I had another name.
I wish I was popular and in a pack
of giggling girls, all the same.

I wish my hair was straight.
I wish my teeth were too.
I wish I could stay up very late.
20 I wish I was you.

Jackie Kay

break in pattern for effect

shorter last line for added impact

Questions

1 | Do you share any of the poet's wishes?
2 | Which wishes (if any) make you feel sorry for the writer?
3 | Are any of the wishes funny?
4 | What patterns are there?

27

Unit 12 : The Iron Man

Main learning objectives

- To understand how writers create imaginary worlds
- To understand how the use of expressive and descriptive language can build tension

Whole class

Introduction

At the beginning of this story, everyone is frightened of the great giant, the Iron Man. But then something even more frightening appears. People notice a star rushing through space and heading for the earth. We are going to read the description of the terrible Space Being. We are going to look at the way in which the writer helps us to imagine how colossal it is. Notice, as well, how the writer uses paragraphs to organize his writing.

Read the extract to the children and discuss it with them. Turn to pages 54–5 for the teacher's version of the text and Questions.

Independent work

Activities: Reading

- Reading Skills A (page 13) or B (page 13).
- To be worked on as an independent exercise.

The drawing activity (of a Space Being) is intended to check comprehension, not to test drawing skills. It should be done with close reference to the text. Make sure that the children do not spend more than a third of the available time on this question.

Guided reading/Extension work

1 Explore how the writer conveys the vast scale by comparing the monster with things we know. Look at a map of the world in an atlas. Find Australia and work out how the body of the Space Being would fit on it (lines 27–30). Read the sentence from lines 30–3. Why didn't all the people who lived in Australia get squashed? Read lines 34–6. Who did get squashed? Look at the enormous distances between Australia, London, California and Russia (lines 18–23). Find Switzerland and compare its size with that of England. Imagine looking out of the classroom window – what would we see? e.g. Just one of its eyes would fill up the whole of. . . Even the moon, 'peered fearfully' (line 15).

2 Compare this passage with the following descriptions of the size of the Iron Man which come earlier in the story: 'a giant black figure, taller than a house'; 'his great iron head, shaped like a dustbin but as big as a bedroom'; 'a foot as big as a single bed'. Point out that the Space Being makes the Iron Man seem quite small! Ask the children to suggest some similes: 'as big as a. . .', 'like a. . .'

Whole class

Plenary discussion

Compare the children's pictures, which are likely to have some significant differences. Everyone's imagination is different. But do the pictures illustrate the words? Look for details of scaly, knobbly skin, horns, claws, fangs, and huge eyes. Have the children indicated the size in any way – e.g. by including an outline of Australia? Discuss why the writer wrote '*indescribably* terrible eyes'. Is it easier to imagine it in your head than to draw it or describe it?

What might the Space Being do next?

Homework

Write some similes, using the starters below. Discourage the children from using cliches – e.g. 'as quiet as a mouse' by suggesting 'Everyone uses that – let's think of something different.'

Try to think of things that nobody has said before!

As fast as a. . . As slow as a. . . As huge as a. . . As tiny as a. . .
As quiet as a. . . As noisy as a. . .

Additional activities

Sentence and word work

1 Spend more time developing the children's understanding of punctuation and paragraphing, continuing from Question 4. Ask the children to count all the paragraphs up to line 25. Draw eight boxes on the board. Together, compose brief notes to sum up the content of each paragraph as you discuss the reasons for having a new paragraph. Point out again the effect of having single line paragraphs. Why is 'Barrrump!' a separate sentence on a line by itself? *(The effect of shock – a jolt.)* What would happen if you joined up some of the short sentences by using commas instead of full stops? *(It would not be so dramatic.)* Look at the contrasting long sentence (lines 25–7) and the way it builds up the picture, growing more and more awful. (An odd sentence, this, as it has no verb.) Look at the use of questions in lines 4 and 38–9. Introduce the word **cliffhanger**.

Activities: Writing

- Writing Skills (page 26) – writing a descriptive passage using adjectives and similes.
- Shared writing (teacher-led) is followed by an independent task.

Questions

1 How does the writer help you to imagine what the Space Being looks like? *(He compares it to all kinds of different things that you may know about already – bat, lizard, black angel, etc.)*

2 Find clues in the text that show how huge the Space Being is? *(Its wings filled most of the sky, eyes as big as Switzerland, covered the whole of Australia, etc.)*

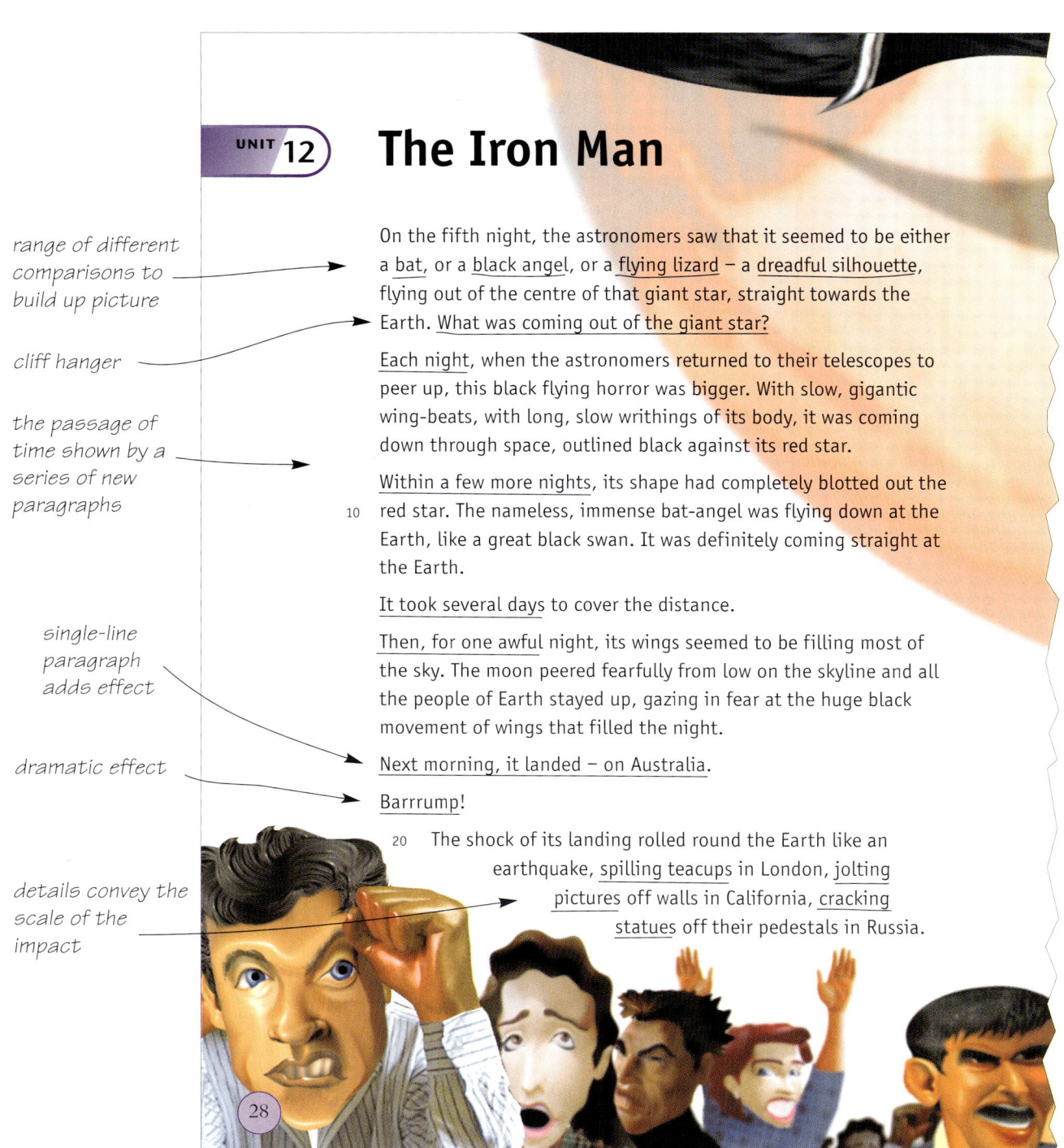

UNIT 12

The Iron Man

range of different comparisons to build up picture

cliff hanger

the passage of time shown by a series of new paragraphs

single-line paragraph adds effect

dramatic effect

details convey the scale of the impact

On the fifth night, the astronomers saw that it seemed to be either a bat, or a black angel, or a flying lizard – a dreadful silhouette, flying out of the centre of that giant star, straight towards the Earth. What was coming out of the giant star?

Each night, when the astronomers returned to their telescopes to peer up, this black flying horror was bigger. With slow, gigantic wing-beats, with long, slow writhings of its body, it was coming down through space, outlined black against its red star.

10 Within a few more nights, its shape had completely blotted out the red star. The nameless, immense bat-angel was flying down at the Earth, like a great black swan. It was definitely coming straight at the Earth.

It took several days to cover the distance.

Then, for one awful night, its wings seemed to be filling most of the sky. The moon peered fearfully from low on the skyline and all the people of Earth stayed up, gazing in fear at the huge black movement of wings that filled the night.

Next morning, it landed – on Australia.

Barrrump!

20 The shock of its landing rolled round the Earth like an earthquake, spilling teacups in London, jolting pictures off walls in California, cracking statues off their pedestals in Russia.

28

3 Why do you think the writer uses the word 'terribly' so many times? *(It builds up the picture of something really terrible!)*

4 **a)** Can you say in one sentence what the first paragraph is about? *(It is about what the astronomers saw on the fifth night.)*

b) What (in one sentence) happens in the second paragraph? *(The flying horror gets nearer.)*

c) Why are there new paragraphs on lines 10, 14, 19, 20 and 25? *(Time has passed. Point out also that line 25 is all by itself because it's a very important moment in the story.)*

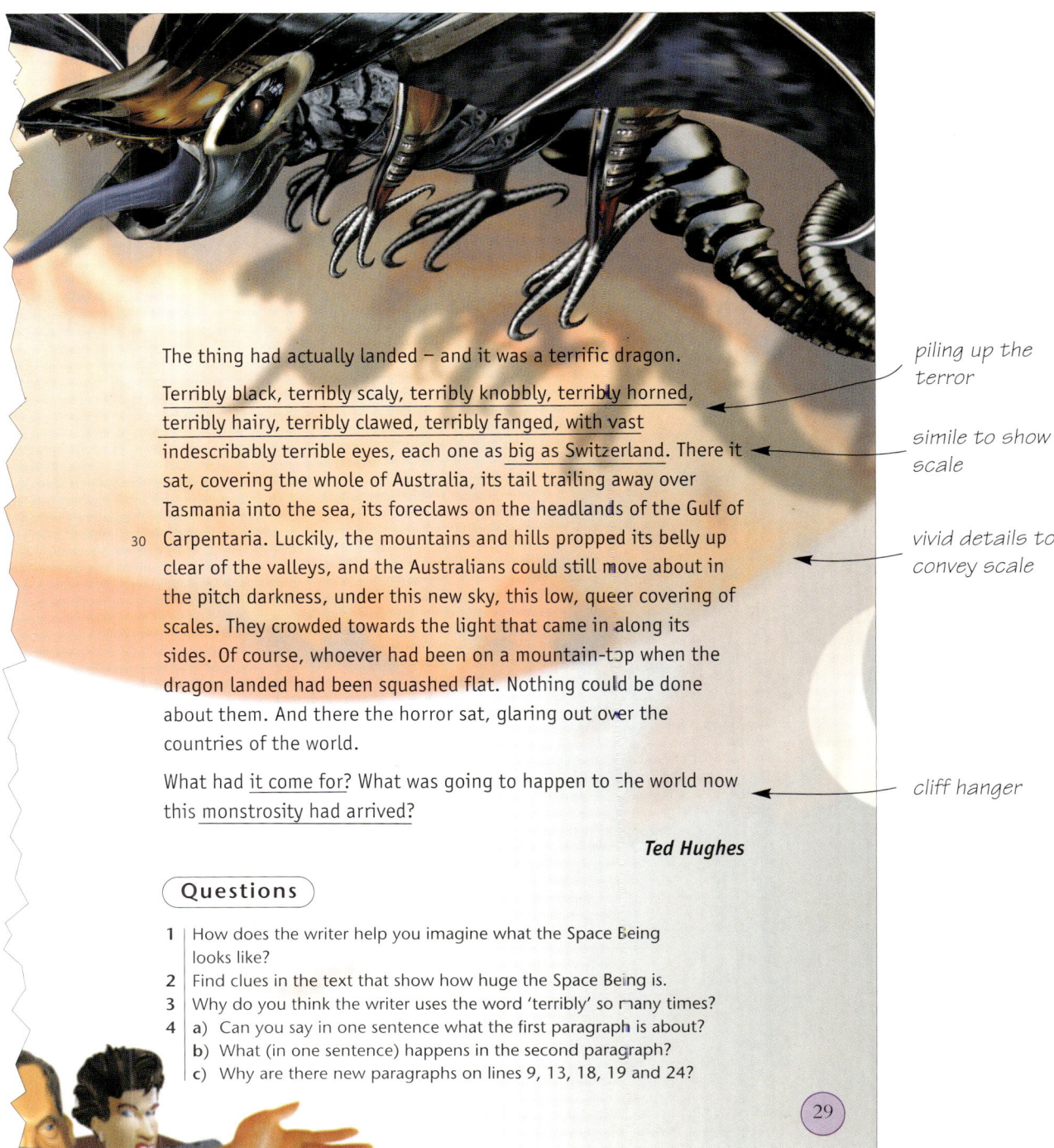

The thing had actually landed – and it was a terrific dragon.

Terribly black, terribly scaly, terribly knobbly, terribly horned, terribly hairy, terribly clawed, terribly fanged, with vast indescribably terrible eyes, each one as big as Switzerland. There it sat, covering the whole of Australia, its tail trailing away over Tasmania into the sea, its foreclaws on the headlands of the Gulf of
30 Carpentaria. Luckily, the mountains and hills propped its belly up clear of the valleys, and the Australians could still move about in the pitch darkness, under this new sky, this low, queer covering of scales. They crowded towards the light that came in along its sides. Of course, whoever had been on a mountain-top when the dragon landed had been squashed flat. Nothing could be done about them. And there the horror sat, glaring out over the countries of the world.

What had it come for? What was going to happen to the world now this monstrosity had arrived?

Ted Hughes

piling up the terror

simile to show scale

vivid details to convey scale

cliff hanger

Questions

1 How does the writer help you imagine what the Space Being looks like?

2 Find clues in the text that show how huge the Space Being is.

3 Why do you think the writer uses the word 'terribly' so many times?

4 **a)** Can you say in one sentence what the first paragraph is about?

 b) What (in one sentence) happens in the second paragraph?

 c) Why are there new paragraphs on lines 9, 13, 18, 19 and 24?

29

Unit 13 : Pompeii – Caught in Time

Main learning objectives

- To identify how and why paragraphs are used to organize information
- To select key words, phrases or sentences when seeking information

Whole class

Introduction

This extract gives information about the town of Pompeii in Italy and what happened there two thousand years ago.

Read the extract to the children and discuss it with them. Turn to pages 58–9 for the teacher's version of the text and Questions.

Independent work

Activities: Reading

- Reading Skills A (page 14) or B (page 14).
- To be worked on in pairs.

Guided reading/Extension work

1 Read the text on **Worksheet 18** (Pompeii). Demonstrate how to extract information. Underline the key words or phrases.
2 Discuss why the local people might not have gone near the ruins of the buried town of Pompeii.

Whole class

Plenary discussion

As a class, re-read the passage. Decide what each paragraph is about, giving a heading to each (e.g., *Introduction, What happened in Pompeii, Pompeii lies forgotten, Archaeologists rediscover Pompeii, What they found, What you can see today*).

Homework

Write and design an advertisement to attract visitors to Pompeii. Use facts and try to make Pompeii sound interesting and exciting. *(You could give them a copy of the text on **Worksheet 19** (Facts about Pompeii).)*

Additional activities

Sentence and word work

1 Compare where (and why) the past and present tense are used. The last paragraph – about Pompeii today – is in the present tense.

2 Discuss the spelling of the past tense -ed. List some words in the past tense under a heading: 'What we did yesterday', e.g. we ran, laughed, joked. List them under words that end in -ed and words that change their spelling.

3 Focus on the use of the apostrophe in 'chariots' wheels'. How many chariots were there? If there was only one chariot where would the apostrophe be? Look for other examples in other texts.

Activities: Writing

- Writing Skills (page 28) – The children need **Worksheet 19** (Facts about Pompeii) – compiling a list of key facts on an information sheet about Pompeii.

- Shared writing (teacher-led) is followed an independent task.

Questions

1 How many facts can you find in the first paragraph? *(Pompeii was a Roman town. It was in Italy. There was a volcanic eruption. It was on 24th August 79 AD, etc.)*

2 Which do you think are the most important? *(Volcanic eruption, in Pompeii, 79 AD are probably the three key pieces of information.)*

UNIT **13**

POMPEII CAUGHT IN TIME

ambiguous title

opening statement with main facts

Pompeii was a Roman town in Italy. On 24th August 79 AD it was caught in an enormous volcanic eruption.

event

Millions of tonnes of lava, pumice and ash shot into the sky. A great cloud hid the sun and there was total darkness for three days and nights. The terrible cloud of dust rained down on the towns around. Pompeii was buried under a
10 blanket of ash and lava that was four to five metres thick and many people were smothered. About 2,000 people lost their lives.

people's reaction

The ruins of Pompeii lay buried for hundreds of years. People who lived nearby did not dare go near where the town had been as they were afraid.

specialists' investigation

Since the last century, archaeologists have been excavating the town. What they have
20 uncovered tells us much about how Roman people used to live.

what they found

Many temples, baths and theatres were discovered. Some had magnificent carvings and statues that were preserved under the ash. Even some brightly coloured wall

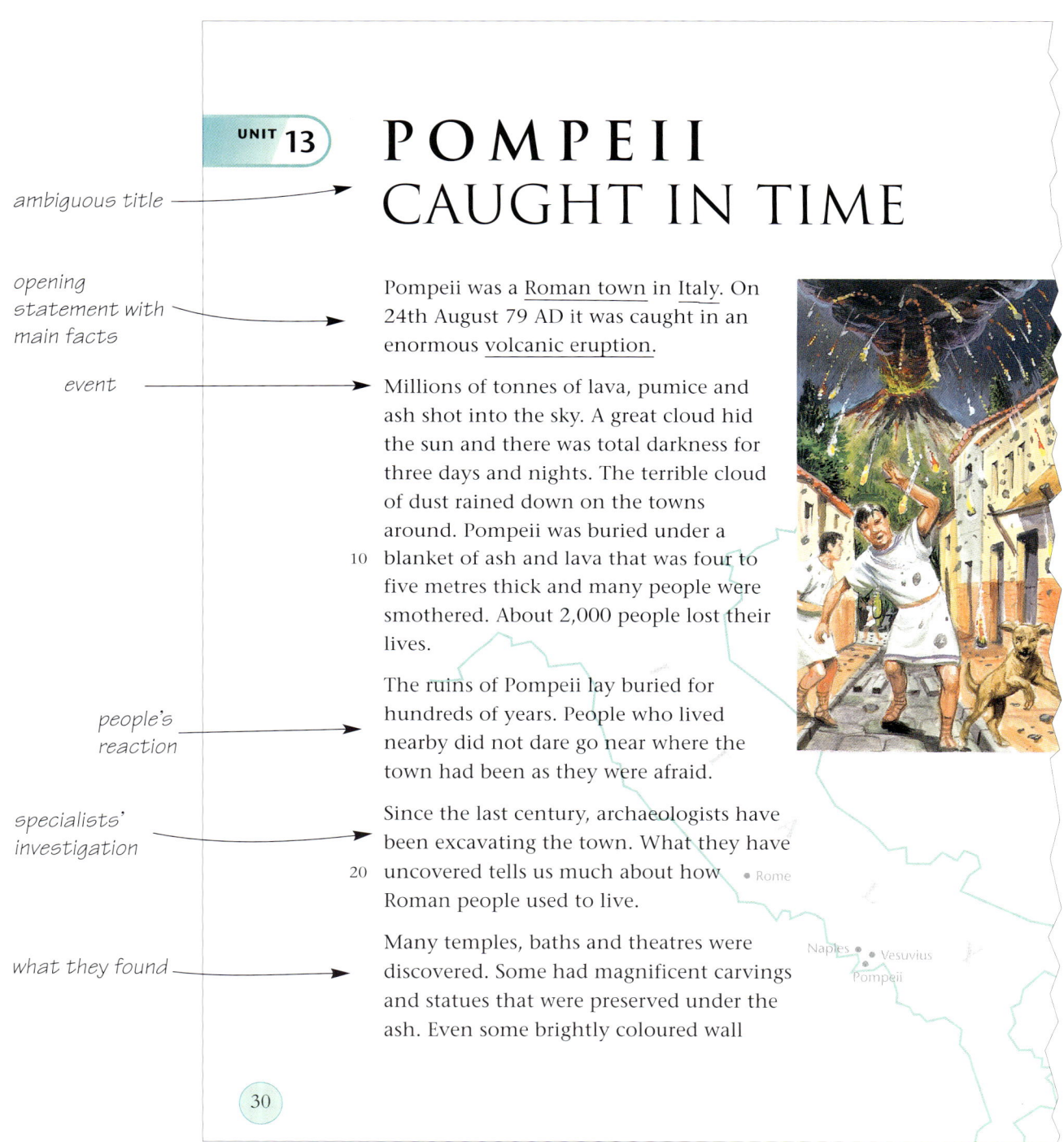

30

paintings had survived. Ordinary shops such as bakeries and cafes were found.

30 You can visit Pompeii nowadays to see the ruins. The streets are still scarred by the ruts left from the chariots' wheels. You can visit the famous amphitheatre where the gladiators fought. You can stand inside the houses and imagine what life was like for the Romans who lived there nearly two thousand years ago.

Boy reading, from a wall painting at the Villa of the Mysteries.

final paragraph relates subject to reader

Ruined Pompeii today, with Vesuvius in the distance.

Questions

1 | How many facts can you find in the first paragraph?
2 | Which do you think are the most important?
3 | Read the second paragraph again. What is the most important information there?

31

Unit 14 : In Wonderland

Main learning objective

● To compare and contrast settings across a range of stories

Whole class

Introduction

Anything can happen in stories. You can get to a magic world with special boots, or down a rabbit hole, or even through a wardrobe. . . These extracts describe different imaginary worlds. We are going to think about how the writer describes the magic places.

The boy in the first extract has seen some amazing boots in a shop window. He tries them on.

Read the first extract to the children and discuss it with them. Turn to page 62 for the teacher's version of the text and Questions.

In the second extract, Alice has just fallen down a rabbit hole – 'down, down, down'. At the bottom she finds herself in a long, dark hall, with locked doors all around it.

Read the second extract to the children and discuss it with them. Turn to page 63 for the teacher's version of the text and Questions.

In the third extract, Lucy is playing hide and seek in her uncle's house. She hides in the wardrobe.

Read the third extract to the children and discuss it with them. Turn to pages 64–5 for the teacher's version of the text and Questions.

Independent work

Activities: Reading

● Reading Skills A (page 15) or B (page 15).
● To be worked on as an independent exercise.

Guided reading/Extension work

Compare 'real 'and 'magic'. *(See also Sentence and word work.)*

1 In the first extract, look at the contrast between reality – 'scraggy socks', 'jeans' – ordinary everyday clothes, and 'magic boots' – warm, bright colours.

2 In the second extract the contrast is of scale – the magic world is miniature – so small that you are too big to get in. Also note the contrast between the dark hall and the bright garden. Do the children know what happens next? How might Alice be able to get into the little garden? If possible, find a copy of 'Alice in Wonderland' and read on to where Alice 'shuts up like a telescope'.

3 In the third extract, look for contrasts between the wardrobe and the magic world. The wardrobe is full of soft warm fur; the magic world is cold, prickly, etc.

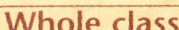

Whole class

Plenary discussion

Look at the use of adjectives in lines 1–6 of the passage from 'Alice in Wonderland'. Can the children think of other adjectives which might have been used to describe the table or the key?

Homework

1 Use **Worksheet 20** (Comparatives and Superlatives).
2 Which of these adjectives can you change to adverbs by adding -ly? big, loud, cross, quiet, small

Extension: Add 'quite', 'more' and 'most' to the adverbs and use them in sentences.

Additional activities

Sentence and word work

1 Adjectives: highlight or make a list of all the adjectives and adjectival phrases in each extract. Illustrate what an **adjectival phrase** is: 'not much larger than a rat-hole' – more than one word, but still describing a noun.

2 Comparatives and superlatives: you can change adjectives by adding -er and -est. Give examples from the Alice extract – 'larger' and 'loveliest'. How does the meaning change – 'large – larger – largest? Can the children supply the adjective and the comparative for the superlative 'loveliest'? Notice the spelling changes.

3 Show how some adjectives can be changed into adverbs to describe a verb, e.g. 'scary – scarily'; 'strange – strangely'; but not 'alien – alienly' or 'long – longly' or 'small – smally'. Discuss why not. If there is time, show how 'quite', 'more' and 'most' can be added to adverbs to alter the intensity, as in comparatives and superlatives above.

Activities: Writing

● Writing Skills (page 30) – writing a description of a magic place.
● Shared writing (teacher-led) is followed by an independent task.

Questions

1 **a)** In the first extract, how could you tell the boots were magic? *(They glowed like fire.)*

b) Where did they take him? *(Up into space.)*

UNIT **14**

In Wonderland

JUPITER BOOTS

contrast with beautiful boots

I pulled the Jupiter boots over my scraggy socks, up and up, over my jeans, up to the knee. Of course they fitted. There had never been any doubt about that. But the warmth of them spread further than my knees; it travelled out to my fingers, swam round my neck and sang in my head.

And then something happened that amazed and frightened me. Fire flickered in my boots. Hot colours swirled over my feet and crawled round my legs. It was like

simile

watching flames caught in a bottle. The Jupiter boots were

10 glowing in the dark. I closed my eyes because it was all so

comparative

scary. And when I did that, ice-cold air rushed over me and the ground slid away. I was flying! Higher and higher and higher. I hugged myself to keep from falling. No one will believe this but I flew past the moon, I know I did. I couldn't

warmth of first part contrasts with chill of second

have dreamed the frost that tingled over my scalp. I couldn't have invented the rumbling of a thousand unknown volcanoes, or the strange smells of alien atmospheres. It was all too scary.

Jenny Nimmo

32

2 What does Alice find in the hall? *(Glass table, tiny key, door to tiny garden.)*

ALICE IN WONDERLAND

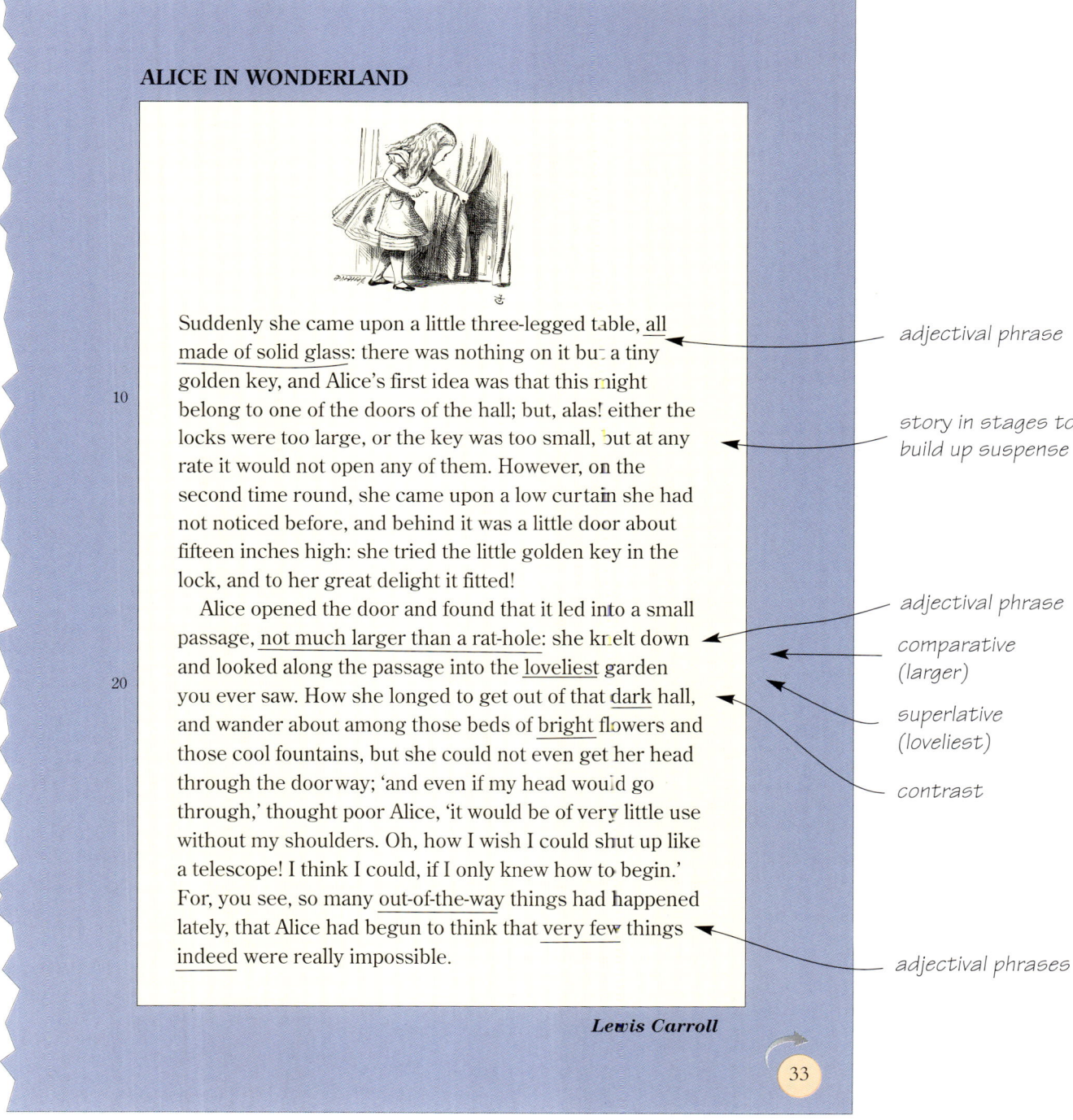

Suddenly she came upon a little three-legged table, all made of solid glass: there was nothing on it but a tiny golden key, and Alice's first idea was that this might belong to one of the doors of the hall; but, alas! either the locks were too large, or the key was too small, but at any rate it would not open any of them. However, on the second time round, she came upon a low curtain she had not noticed before, and behind it was a little door about fifteen inches high: she tried the little golden key in the lock, and to her great delight it fitted!

    Alice opened the door and found that it led into a small passage, not much larger than a rat-hole: she knelt down and looked along the passage into the loveliest garden you ever saw. How she longed to get out of that dark hall, and wander about among those beds of bright flowers and those cool fountains, but she could not even get her head through the doorway; 'and even if my head would go through,' thought poor Alice, 'it would be of very little use without my shoulders. Oh, how I wish I could shut up like a telescope! I think I could, if I only knew how to begin.' For, you see, so many out-of-the-way things had happened lately, that Alice had begun to think that very few things indeed were really impossible.

Lewis Carroll

33

10

20

adjectival phrase

story in stages to build up suspense

adjectival phrase

comparative (larger)

superlative (loveliest)

contrast

adjectival phrases

3 What is unusual about the wardrobe in the third
extract? *(It doesn't have a back – it leads to a
wood.)*

THE LION, THE WITCH AND THE WARDROBE

Looking into the inside, she saw several coats hanging up –
mostly long fur coats. There was nothing Lucy liked so much
as the smell and feel of fur. She immediately stepped into the
wardrobe and got in among the coats and rubbed her face
against them, leaving the door open, of course, because she
knew that it is very foolish to shut oneself into any wardrobe.
Soon she went further in and found that there was a second
row of coats hanging up behind the first one. It was almost
quite dark in there and she kept her arms stretched out in
10 front of her so as not to bump her face into the back of the
wardrobe. She took a step further in – then two or three steps
– always expecting to feel woodwork against the tips of her
fingers. But she could not feel it.

'This must be a simply enormous wardrobe!' thought Lucy,
going still further in and pushing the soft folds of the coats
aside to make room for her. Then she noticed that there was
something crunching under her feet. 'I wonder is that more
mothballs?' she thought, stooping down to feel it with her
hand. But instead of feeling the hard, smooth wood of the
20 floor of the wardrobe, she felt something soft and powdery
and extremely cold. 'This is very queer,' she said, and went
on a step or two further.

*build up of
suspense*

*contrast to
snow*

clues to snow

34

4 **a)** Which adventure would you choose to be in?
   b) Do you know any other stories about magic
      places or objects? *(The children may know the
      'Magic Key' stories in the Oxford Reading Tree, or
      'Jack and the Beanstalk'.)*

    Next moment, she found that what was rubbing against her
face and hands was no longer <u>soft fur</u> but something <u>hard and
rough</u> and even <u>prickly</u>. 'Why, it is just like branches of trees!'
exclaimed Lucy. And then she saw that there was <u>a light ahead</u>
of her; not a few inches away where the back of the wardrobe
ought to have been, but a long way off. Something cold and
soft was falling on her. A moment later she found that she was
30 standing in the middle of a wood at night-time with snow
under her feet and snowflakes falling through the air.

                                                    C. S. Lewis

contrasts

clues to wood

clue to night time

Questions

1 **a)** In the first extract, how could you tell the boots were magic?
   b) Where did they take him?
2 What does Alice find in the hall?
3 What is unusual about the wardrobe in the third extract?
4 **a)** Which adventure would you choose to be in?
   b) Do you know any other stories about magic things or places?

35

Unit 15 : Storytime

Main learning objectives

- To read and interpret a conversation poem
- To consider how best to read a poem
- To discuss typical features of a poem

Whole class

Introduction

This poem is by Judith Nicholls. When we read it through you will be able to tell that she was once a teacher. She now makes her living as a full-time writer. She visits lots of schools and gives poetry readings and runs writers' workshops.

Read the poem to the children and discuss it with them. Turn to pages 68–9 for the teacher's version of the text and Questions.

Independent work

Activities: Reading

- Reading Skills A (page 16) or B (page 16).
- To be worked on in pairs.

Guided reading/Extension work

1 With a group of lower attainers, work together to read the poem with expression. Comment on each other's readings. You may want to use **Worksheet 21** (Evaluation Sheet).

2 Identify and list the adjectives. Change these for other adjectives and discuss the effect this has on the poem.

Whole class

Plenary discussion

1 Talk about who is 'telling a story'. *(In a way, they are all telling stories. We know the poet and the teacher are. It is less clear whether Andrew is.)*

2 Ask several children to read the poem aloud.

Homework

Write Andrew's diary describing what happened in the classroom.
Or

Write the conversation between the teacher and another teacher about what happened. Think about what happened after the end of the poem.

Additional activities

Sentence and word work

Invent together other similes, using 'as', such as:

    as tall as
    as thin as
    as slim as
    as cold as
    as clean as
    as dark as

The children may offer well-known phrases. Introduce the idea of the cliché – a phrase or expression that has been over-used. Try inventing new similes, for example:

as slow as a snail with its brakes on

as thin as the edge of a razor blade on a slimming diet.

Activities: Writing

- Writing Skills (page 32) – writing the conversation poem as if it was narrative.
- Shared writing (teacher-led) is followed by an independent task.

Questions

1 Is the dragon real? *(We don't know. – At the end it is suggested that there is a real dragon. – 'I did try to tell you, miss.' At the beginning we are told 'Jamie's made a dragon out in the sandpit'. The children may suggest that Andrew has made it up.)*

2 a) How can you tell when Andrew is talking? *(His words are written in italics – look at the difference between how the teacher speaks and how Andrew speaks – his words are colloquial, she uses more poetic, story language.)*

b) Is Andrew trying to be helpful? *(Most children will say – yes; some may suggest that they think that he often butts in when the teacher is talking.)*

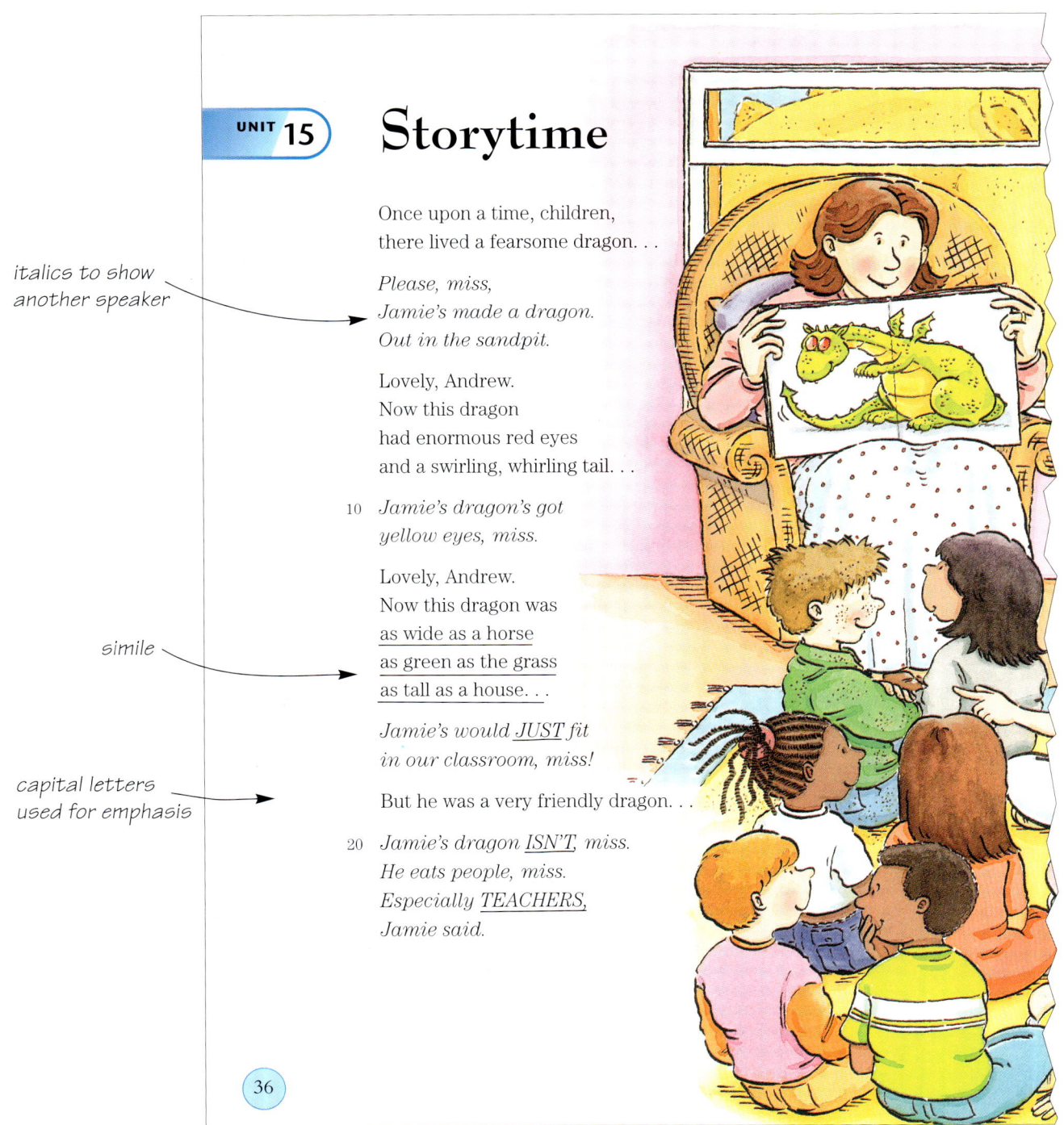

UNIT 15

Storytime

Once upon a time, children,
there lived a fearsome dragon. . .

Please, miss,
Jamie's made a dragon.
Out in the sandpit.

italics to show
another speaker

Lovely, Andrew.
Now this dragon
had enormous red eyes
and a swirling, whirling tail. . .

10 *Jamie's dragon's got*
yellow eyes, miss.

Lovely, Andrew.
Now this dragon was
as wide as a horse
as green as the grass
as tall as a house. . .

simile

Jamie's would JUST fit
in our classroom, miss!

But he was a very friendly dragon. . .

capital letters
used for emphasis

20 *Jamie's dragon ISN'T, miss.*
He eats people, miss.
Especially TEACHERS,
Jamie said.

36

3 How does the teacher treat Andrew? *(She is really ignoring him – but she cannot be blamed, after all he is suggesting that there is a dragon in the sandpit!)*

4 The poet used to be a teacher. Can you spot any words or phrases that she might have used in class *('Lovely Andrew, very nice, thank you. . .' stereotypical phrases that some infant teachers use. Can the children say them in the same way as a teacher might?)*

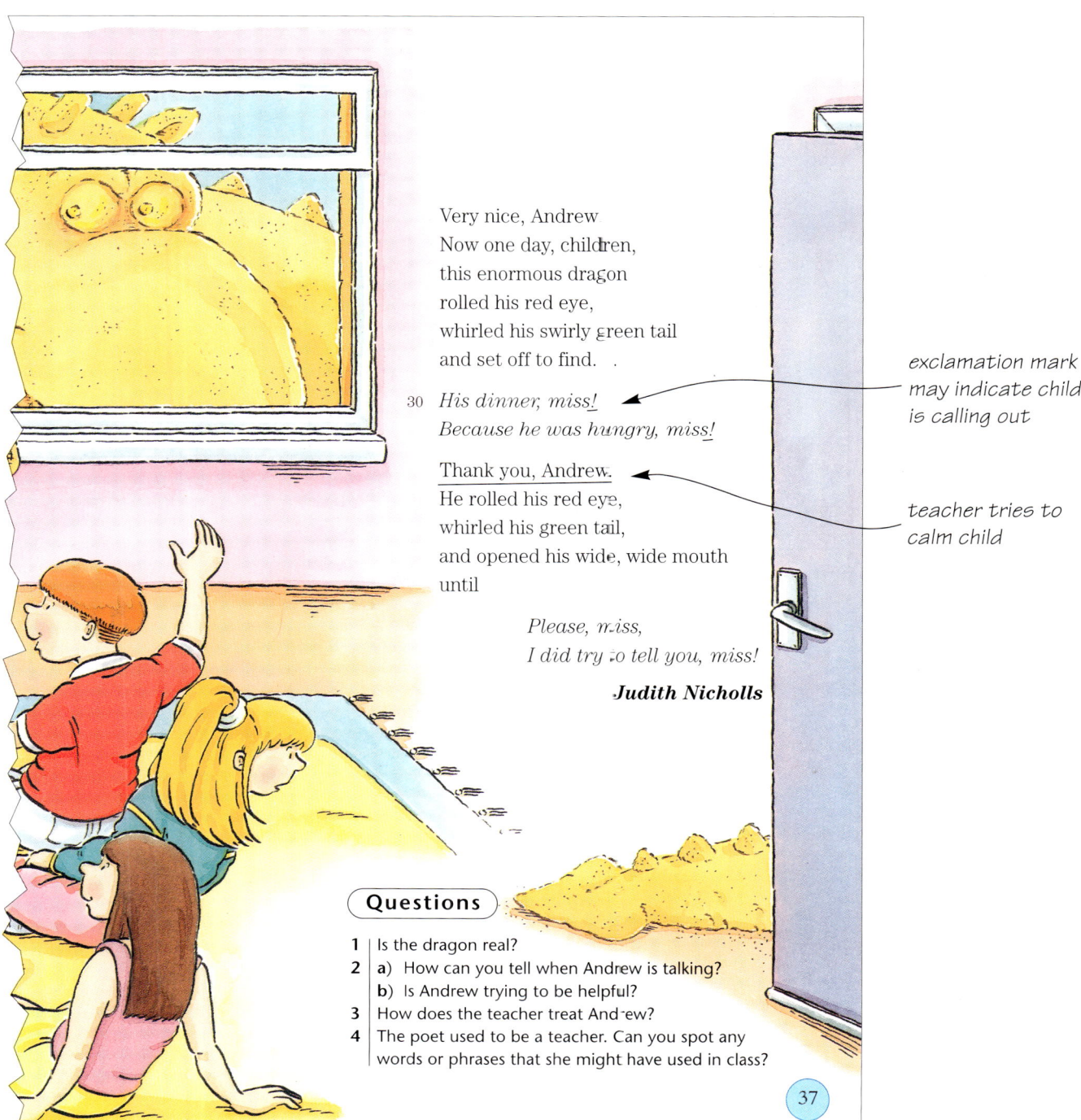

Very nice, Andrew
Now one day, children,
this enormous dragon
rolled his red eye,
whirled his swirly green tail
and set off to find. .

30 *His dinner, miss!*
Because he was hungry, miss!

Thank you, Andrew.
He rolled his red eye,
whirled his green tail,
and opened his wide, wide mouth
until

    Please, miss,
    I did try to tell you, miss!

Judith Nicholls

exclamation mark may indicate child is calling out

teacher tries to calm child

Questions

1 Is the dragon real?
2 **a)** How can you tell when Andrew is talking?
   b) Is Andrew trying to be helpful?
3 How does the teacher treat Andrew?
4 The poet used to be a teacher. Can you spot any words or phrases that she might have used in class?

37

Unit 16 : Hot Air Balloons

Main learning objective

● To identify the key features of explanatory texts: purpose, structure, language and presentation

Whole class

Introduction

As we read through this piece of writing, think carefully about its purpose. Who would want or need to read such a piece of writing. What might it help you do? Think also about what each paragraph is telling the reader.

Read the piece of writing to the children and discuss it with them. Turn to pages 72–3 for the teacher's version of the text and Questions.

Independent work

Activities: Reading

● Reading Skills A (page 17) or B (page 17).
● To be worked on as an independent exercise.

Guided reading/Extension work

1 What other illustrations, with captions, would you add to show children younger than you how to make a hot air balloon?

2 Where else do you see or need texts which explain things? *(Distinguish between:*

   i) instructions which tell you how to do things, e.g. recipes, how to play a game

   ii) explanations which tell you how and why they work, explaining a process or answering a question.)

3 Re-read the passage and find words or phrases that would be useful for either kind of explanation, e.g. How to make, you need, you also need, so this causes, if you, because. . .

Whole class

Plenary discussion

1 Look again at the writing frame that shows how the text is structured. Decide on simple headings that everyone understands.

2 Discuss which sentence is the most important – without which you would not be able to explain or understand how a hot air balloon rises.

Homework

Worksheet 22 (Growing Cress) contains a set of brief notes. Use it to write an explanation. Use complete sentences and paragraphs.

Additional activities

Sentence and word work

1 What tense are the verbs in? *(Mainly present tense.)*
2 Where do they usually come in the sentences? *(Near the start of the sentences.)*
3 Look carefully at the part which is an explanation. Which are the key words which could be used in many explanatory texts? *(This causes. . .)*

Activities: Writing

● Writing Skills (page 34) – picking key information out of a text.
● Shared writing (teacher-led) is followed by an independent task.

1. What is the purpose of the piece of writing? *(It explains how to make a simple hot air balloon and how a hot air balloon works.)*

2. Who might read it and why? *(A child who wants to know how to make a hot air balloon and someone who wants to know how they fly.)*

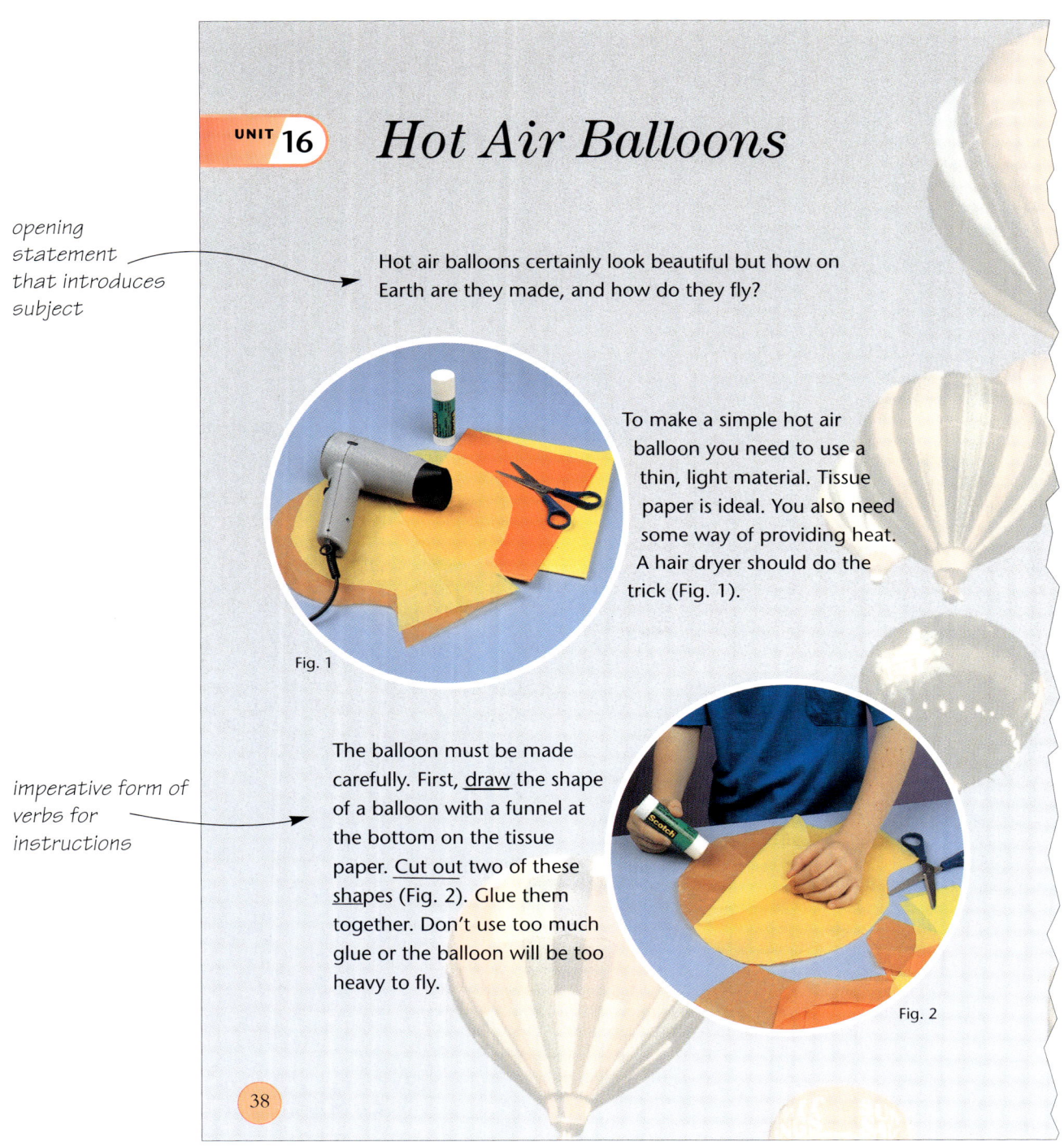

UNIT 16

Hot Air Balloons

opening statement that introduces subject

Hot air balloons certainly look beautiful but how on Earth are they made, and how do they fly?

To make a simple hot air balloon you need to use a thin, light material. Tissue paper is ideal. You also need some way of providing heat. A hair dryer should do the trick (Fig. 1).

Fig. 1

imperative form of verbs for instructions

The balloon must be made carefully. First, <u>draw</u> the shape of a balloon with a funnel at the bottom on the tissue paper. <u>Cut out</u> two of these shapes (Fig. 2). Glue them together. Don't use too much glue or the balloon will be too heavy to fly.

Fig. 2

38

3 Make up a heading for each paragraph. *(Ask the children to read each paragraph in turn. Ask them what the paragraph tells us. Encourage them to create a writing frame in five parts:*

1 *Introduction – What you are trying to explain.*
2 *Materials – What you need.*
3 *First things to do.*
4 *How to make it work – Explanation of how it works.*
5 *General information.)*

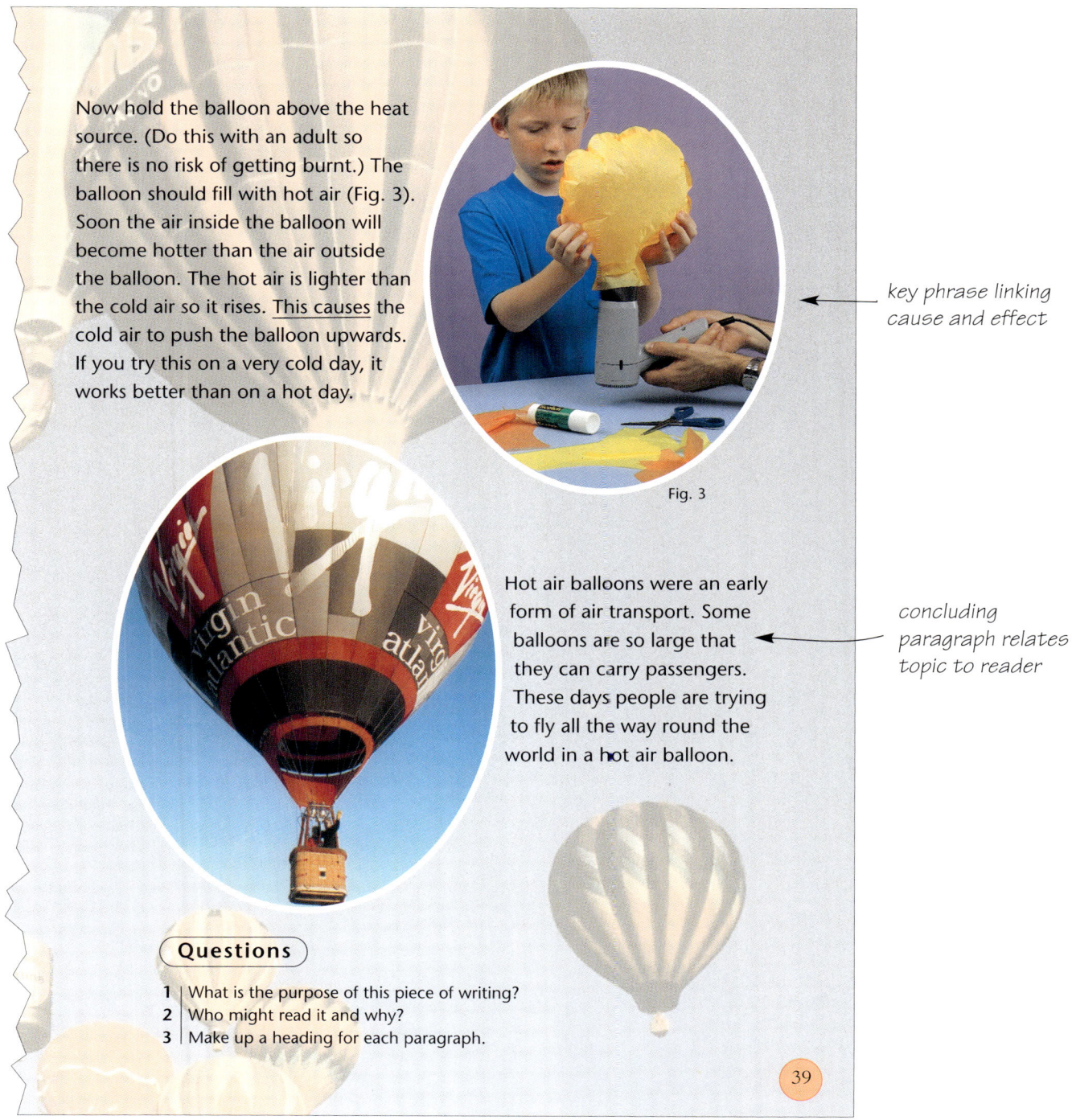

Now hold the balloon above the heat source. (Do this with an adult so there is no risk of getting burnt.) The balloon should fill with hot air (Fig. 3). Soon the air inside the balloon will become hotter than the air outside the balloon. The hot air is lighter than the cold air so it rises. <u>This causes</u> the cold air to push the balloon upwards. If you try this on a very cold day, it works better than on a hot day.

key phrase linking cause and effect

Fig. 3

Hot air balloons were an early form of air transport. Some balloons are so large that they can carry passengers. These days people are trying to fly all the way round the world in a hot air balloon.

concluding paragraph relates topic to reader

Questions

1 What is the purpose of this piece of writing?
2 Who might read it and why?
3 Make up a heading for each paragraph.

39

Unit 17 : Lullaby

Main learning objectives

- To identify the use of repetitive patterns and consider their impact
- To appreciate the use of poetic phrasing

Whole class

Introduction

This poem is a translation of a song sung by the people of the Gabon. The idea of the lullaby is that the listener should fall asleep by the end.

Read the poem to the children and discuss it with them. Turn to page 76 for the teacher's version of the text and Questions.

Independent work

Activities: Reading

- Reading Skills A (page 18) or B (page 18).
- To be worked on as an independent exercise.

Guided reading/Extension work

1 Change the poem by turning it into a morning song. Look at each line and change it. For instance, you could begin by writing:

   'Wake, wake, little one, open your eyes, wake little one!'

2 Change some of the 'poetic' lines into what the mother might actually say to her child. For instance, look at the line 'on your closed eyes day has fled'. What words might the mother have really said?

3 Find a clue that tells the reader that this lullaby was written in another country.

Whole class

Plenary discussion

Share ideas for what the last line might mean – both Reading Skills books end by asking the children to discuss this. We cannot know exactly what the singer is thinking. Tomorrow is important for the child. The future belongs to the child as they grow up – but mother (or mother's love) will always be there.

Discuss what picture the poem makes in your head – what do the children see?

Homework

Use **Worksheet 23** (Lullaby Cloze). The children should read through and decide what might be the most appropriate words to fit into the lullaby. They can then illustrate it.

Additional activities

Sentence and word work

1   Re-read the poem and list the verbs. Make three columns – past, present and future – and fill in each column for each verb, for example:

Past	Present	Future
slept	sleep	will sleep
came	come	will come
etc.		

2   Suggest another word for 'comes' in line 3, 'closed' in line 5 and 'take' in line 11.

Activities: Writing

● Writing Skills (page 36) – writing a lullaby, using this poem as a model.

● Shared writing (teacher-led) is followed by an independent task.

1. Do you think the 'little one' might be a boy or a girl? *('You will be big, you will be strong' and 'you will take the bow and the knife' suggest that the child is a boy. Explore this. – Do we want the same kinds of things from boys as this African poet does?)*

2. Find a clue that suggests the time of day. *(Ask the children to search for clues. 'The night comes down', tells us that it is evening.)*

3. What does the poet mean by the phrase 'and I bent'? *(The singer suggests that when the child has grown tall, the singer will be hunched with age. We can infer that 'tomorrow' not only means the next day but also the distant future.)*

4. When the poem is read aloud, what helps to make it sound sleepy? *(The repetitions have a soothing effect, the words sound comforting and safe, etc.)*

UNIT 17

Lullaby

repeated throughout for effect

Sleep, sleep, little one, close your eyes, sleep, little one!
The night comes down, the hour has come, tomorrow it will be day.

milk

Sleep, sleep little one! On your closed eyes day has fled.
You are warm. You have drunk, sleep, sleep, little one!

the future

Sleep, tomorrow you will be big, you will be strong.

suggests another culture

Sleep, tomorrow you will take the bow and the knife.
Sleep, you will be strong, you will be straight, and I bent.

bent with age

Sleep, tomorrow it is you, but it is mother always.

African poem from Gabon

Questions

1. Do you think the 'little one' is a boy or a girl?
2. Find a clue that suggests the time of day.
3. What is meant by the phrase, 'and I bent'?
4. When the poem is read aloud what helps to make it sound sleepy?

40

enigmatic conclusion

Unit 18 : Junior Horror

Main learning objectives

- To identify themes
- To recognize how certain types of text are targeted at particular readers

Whole class

Introduction

Have you read any books from a horror story series? They are very popular. The two extracts here are from the 'Goosebumps' series. We are going to look at what they have in common, and why they are popular with readers of about your age.

In the first extract, the children are suspicious about their new teacher, who seems to have some secret. They follow her into Fear Street Cemetery, and in the dark they fall into a grave. They manage to climb out, but there's another shock waiting for them. . .

Read the extract from 'Ghosts of Fear Street' to the children and discuss it with them. Turn to page 79 for the teacher's version of the texts and Questions.

In the second extract, the children discover an Abominable Snowman, who is not very friendly. . .

Read the extract from 'The Abominable Snowman of Pasadena' to the children and discuss it with them. Turn to pages 80–81 for the teacher's version of the texts and Questions.

Independent work

Activities: Reading

- Reading Skills A (page 19) or B (page 19).
- Children working on Reading Skills A will need **Worksheet 24** (Horror Story Ingredients).

Guided reading/Extension work

1 Study the recurring verbs: 'cried' and 'screamed'. Use a thesaurus make a list of alternatives: e.g. 'yelled', 'shrieked', 'bellowed'. All the speech is either very loud or very quiet! Think of some more quiet verbs to add to 'whispered': e.g. 'muttered', 'mumbled', 'murmured'. Which fit these horror stories and which do not? Play with the text by substituting verbs and reading with appropriate expression.

2 We don't find out much about what the Abominable Snowman looks like in the second extract. Compare this with the detail in the description of the Space Being in the extract from the 'Iron Man' (Unit 12). Make up a much fuller description of the Abominable Snowman.

Whole class

Plenary discussion

Share the ingredients for horror stories and add further ideas if necessary. Take a vote on favourites, as preparation for Shared writing.

Homework

Arrange these adjectives in order of intensity:

- frightened, scared, worried, jittery, nervous, petrified, horrified, shocked.
- hot, warm, cold, lukewarm, chilly, icy, freezing
- big, enormous, colossal, huge, large, immense, vast.

(Select according to the children's attainment.)

Additional activities

Sentence and word work

1 a) Read the first extract, looking at the short, jerky sentences. Try joining them up to make longer sentences. What effect does it have? Are short sentences better at building up suspense? Are they easier to read?

   b) Is 'Trying to find a clue to guide us' a complete sentence? Does it make sense on its own? It's more like speech, where you often leave things out. It follows on from the sentence before. It it were a complete sentence it would not sound so breathless.

2 Look at the adjectives describing the snowman – what does 'abominable' mean? Look it up. 'Furry' (line 25) doesn't sound very scary, quite cuddly, in fact! Think up some alternatives, e.g. 'ferocious'. Find others, such as 'cross', 'angry', 'furious', 'savage', 'fierce'. Arrange these words in order of intensity.

Activities: Writing

- Writing Skills (page 38) – writing a 'junior' horror story.
- Shared writing (teacher-led) is followed by an independent task.

1 Horror stories often have similar things in them, like ingredients for a horror story recipe. What are some of the ingredients in these extracts? (*Beasts, chases, graveyards, ghosts.*)

2 Can you think of any more from other stories you know? (*Dark, being lost, etc.*)

new paragraphs of very short sentences give jerky, dramatic effect

UNIT **18**

Junior Horror

from GHOSTS OF FEAR STREET

Marcy was staring at a gravestone. The gravestone at the head of the empty grave.

It was very old.

I could barely make out the engraving.

I moved up close to it, squinted, and read:

10   EVANGELINE GAUNT
        BORN 1769 • DIED 1845
        REST IN PEACE

'It's *her* grave!' I screamed. We were in *her* grave!

'She is a ghost!' I cried. 'Let's get out of here. Before she finds us!'

We charged through the cemetery, stumbling over rocks and dodging graves.

We ran and ran. But we were
20 nowhere near the entrance.

'It's a maze!' Marcy cried. 'We're going around in circles.'

I stopped. My eyes darted left and right. Trying to find a clue to guide us.

The mist began to lift, and I spotted some hedges a few feet away. 'Let's go through there!' I cried.

I parted the hedges and held them back so Marcy could squeeze through. The little thorns ripped into my hands. But I didn't care.

As I shoved through the hedge after Marcy, I yelled, 'Look! The entrance! We're almost there!'

We dashed to the gates, jumped on our bikes, and pedalled as hard as we could. We didn't speak until we reached Marcy's house.

'Now do you believe me?'

Marcy nodded, gasping for breath. 'Miss Gaunt is a ghost. What are we going to do?'

I wiped the sweat from my forehead. 'We have to tell the rest of the kids as soon as we reach school tomorrow,' I said. 'Meet me outside the main entrance at eight-fifteen. We'll catch them before they go in – and warn them. . .

urgent verbs

short incomplete sentences give breathless effect

urgent verbs

3 How does the writer keep you on the edge of your seat? *(Cliffhangers – will they escape? – short sentences, lots of exclamation marks and question marks.)*

4 What do you like about horror stories?

dramatic opening

exclamation mark indicates drama

action verbs

urgent verbs and short sentences

from THE ABOMINABLE SNOWMAN OF PASADENA

Crack!

The block of ice splintered apart. Nicole and I pressed ourselves against a wall, watching with horror.

The Abominable Snowman burst from the ice. Chunks of ice smashed on the floor and shattered like glass. The snowman shook himself, growling like a wolf.

'Run!' I screamed.

Nicole and I took off. But there was nowhere to go. We stumbled to the other side of the cave – as far away from the monster as we could get.

'The passageway!' I cried. I ducked down and started to crawl through the passage.

Nicole grabbed me.

'Wait! It's blocked! The avalanche – remember?'

Yes. Of course. The way out of the cave was blocked by tons of snow.

Across the cave, the monster uttered a ferocious roar that shook the walls.

10

42

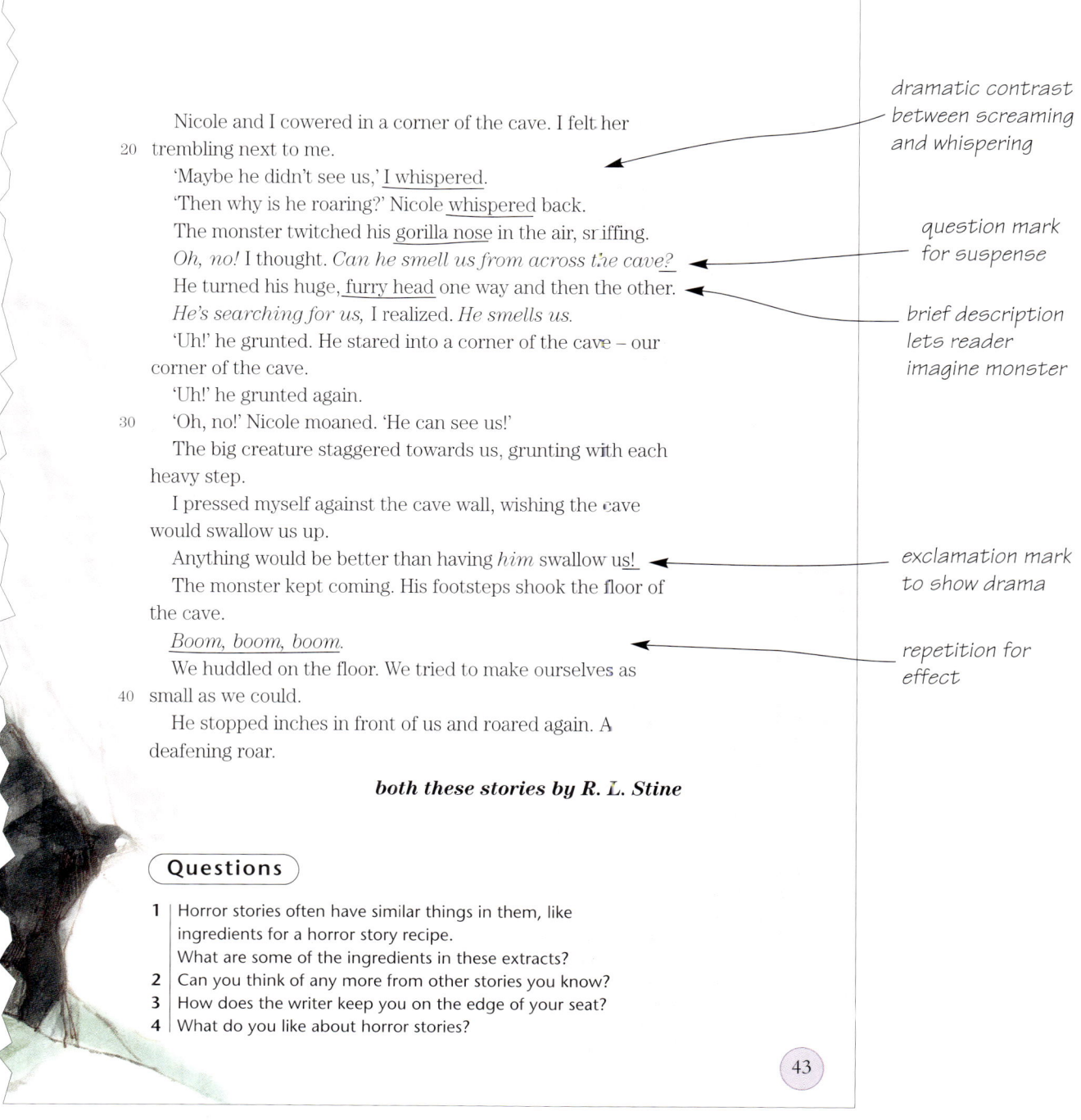

Nicole and I cowered in a corner of the cave. I felt her
20 trembling next to me.

'Maybe he didn't see us,' I whispered.

'Then why is he roaring?' Nicole whispered back.

The monster twitched his gorilla nose in the air, sniffing.

Oh, no! I thought. *Can he smell us from across the cave?*

He turned his huge, furry head one way and then the other.

He's searching for us, I realized. *He smells us.*

'Uh!' he grunted. He stared into a corner of the cave – our
corner of the cave.

'Uh!' he grunted again.

30 'Oh, no!' Nicole moaned. 'He can see us!'

The big creature staggered towards us, grunting with each
heavy step.

I pressed myself against the cave wall, wishing the cave
would swallow us up.

Anything would be better than having *him* swallow us!

The monster kept coming. His footsteps shook the floor of
the cave.

Boom, boom, boom.

We huddled on the floor. We tried to make ourselves as
40 small as we could.

He stopped inches in front of us and roared again. A
deafening roar.

both these stories by R. L. Stine

dramatic contrast between screaming and whispering

question mark for suspense

brief description lets reader imagine monster

exclamation mark to show drama

repetition for effect

(**Questions**)

1 | Horror stories often have similar things in them, like
ingredients for a horror story recipe.
What are some of the ingredients in these extracts?

2 | Can you think of any more from other stories you know?

3 | How does the writer keep you on the edge of your seat?

4 | What do you like about horror stories?

43

Unit 19 : A Walk Down the Pier

Main learning objective

● To explore difficult issues and alternative courses of action

Introduction

We are going to read part of a story where the hero has to face a really difficult challenge. The story is called 'A Walk Down the Pier', written by John Escott.

Davy's friend, old Mr Pennyquick, works at a seaside funfair on the end of the old, rickety pier. One stormy evening, when Davy is helping him with some painting, and everyone else has gone home, Mr Pennyquick falls off the ladder. . .

Read the extract to the children and discuss it with them. Turn to pages 84–5 for the teacher's version of the text and Questions.

Independent work

Activities: Reading

● Reading Skills A (page 20) or B (page 20).
● To be worked on as an independent exercise.

Guided reading/Extension work

1 Why does Davy tell himself 'it's just a walk down the pier' (line 50)? What do you think he is feeling? How would he say those words to himself? How would he speak the words on line 11?

   If he's got to walk down the pier, is it sensible to leave his anorak behind?

2 What would the main dangers be and what should he do to be as safe as possible? What else could he have done? Read lines 36–7 for a clue.

3 At first it was quiet inside the building – scan the extract for clues that tell you this. Then what sounds did Davy hear? (lines 15–18, 42–4). How would the sounds make him feel? Look at examples in the extract which tell us what his thoughts are, for example the question on lines 22–3.

4 Find examples of all the little details Davy notices, because he is so tense with the shock. For example, he notices Mr Pennyquick's chest (line 2) his own croaky voice, the scrape of his foot. . . Discuss what the children have noticed in moments of shock they may have experienced.

Whole class

Plenary discussion

Discuss the pros and cons of what Davy decided to do. Discuss alternative actions he could have taken. Vote on whether he should have done it or not. How might the story continue? Would it have changed our opinion of Davy if he had not gone for help?

Homework

Design a Safety poster warning people about the dangers of going on an old rickety pier.

(Discuss the key points beforehand, e.g.: hold on to the rail, don't go alone, do not go in bad weather or at night, children must be accompanied.)

Or

Think about these questions. Write a paragraph or make notes for a class discussion.

1 If Davy had not gone to get help, what else could he have done?

2 How might the story have ended if he had not gone for help?

Additional activities

Sentence and word work

1 Punctuation: look at the use of a dash on line 2, and at the incomplete sentences that follow. They are like speech; he is thinking to himself. Ask the children to supply the missing words. Look at the dash on line 9, giving emphasis by pausing before 'alone'.

2 Paragraphing: revise the use of paragraphs to show time passing. Chart Davy's actions in each paragraph. Look at connectives, e.g. 'And now', 'Next', 'Afterwards'. Why are the words on line 24 on a line by themselves?

3 Extending words: Look at the adverb 'carefully' on line 34. Ask the children to supply the related adjective and noun. Do the same with the adjective 'comfortable' – supply the noun and adverb. 'Care' and 'comfort' can be used as verbs as well as nouns. Ask the children to use them as verbs in sentences. Look at 'comforting' on line 47. Try adding -ing to 'care'.

Activities: Writing

● Writing Skills (page 40) – Writing a story about a dangerous adventure.

● Shared writing (teacher-led) is followed by an independent task.

Questions

1 How can you tell that Davy is scared? *(He has to force himself to go and look at Mr Pennyquick, his voice croaks, he shudders when he thinks of the pier.)*

2 **a)** What does he do to help Mr Pennyquick? *(Keeps him warm, makes a pillow, goes to get help.)*

b) Are they sensible things to do? What would you have done? *(Yes, they are. Encourage children to engage with the story.)*

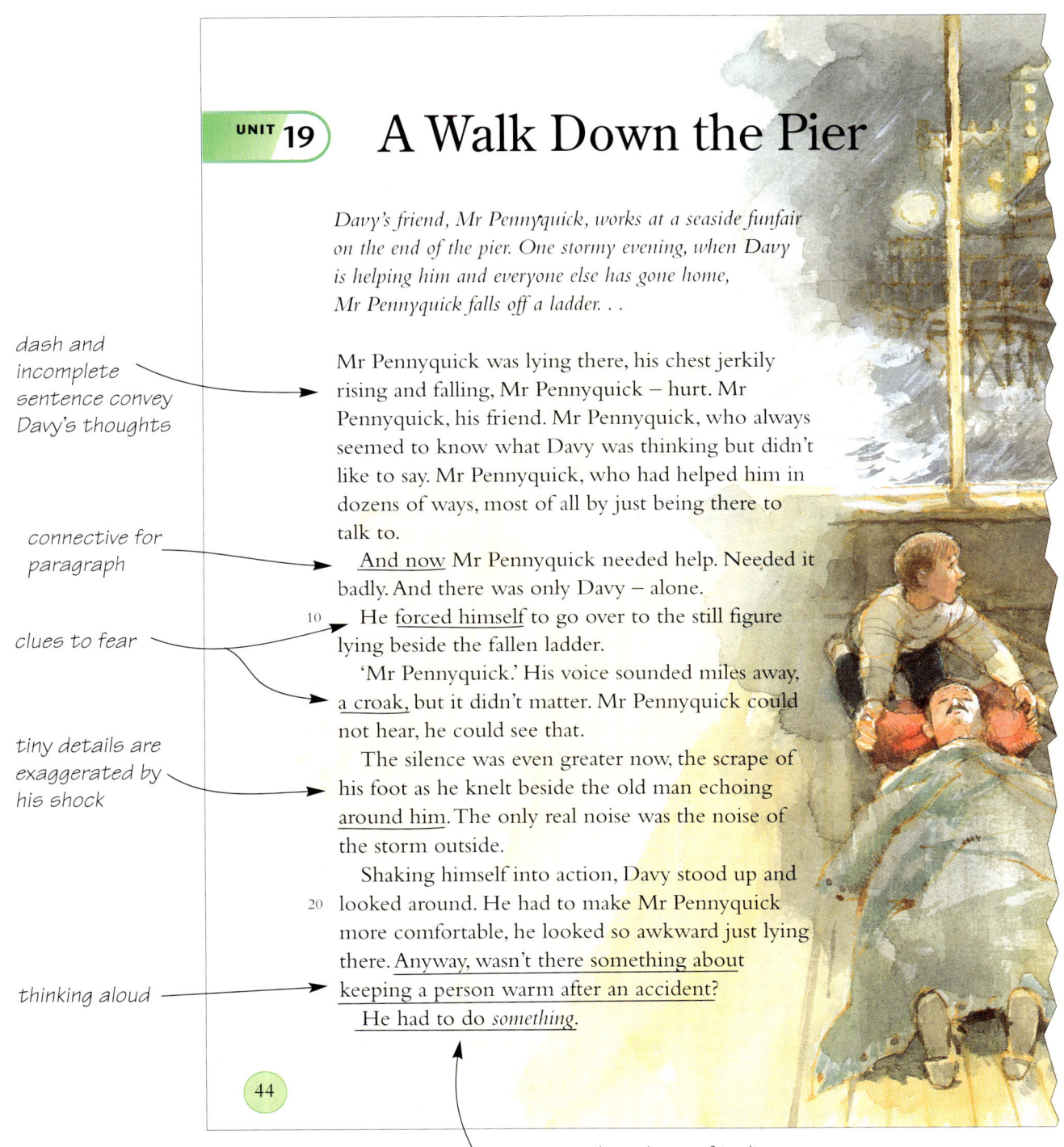

UNIT **19**

A Walk Down the Pier

Davy's friend, Mr Pennyquick, works at a seaside funfair on the end of the pier. One stormy evening, when Davy is helping him and everyone else has gone home, Mr Pennyquick falls off a ladder. . .

Mr Pennyquick was lying there, his chest jerkily rising and falling, Mr Pennyquick – hurt. Mr Pennyquick, his friend. Mr Pennyquick, who always seemed to know what Davy was thinking but didn't like to say. Mr Pennyquick, who had helped him in dozens of ways, most of all by just being there to talk to.

And now Mr Pennyquick needed help. Needed it badly. And there was only Davy – alone.

10 He forced himself to go over to the still figure lying beside the fallen ladder.

'Mr Pennyquick.' His voice sounded miles away, a croak, but it didn't matter. Mr Pennyquick could not hear, he could see that.

The silence was even greater now, the scrape of his foot as he knelt beside the old man echoing around him. The only real noise was the noise of the storm outside.

Shaking himself into action, Davy stood up and
20 looked around. He had to make Mr Pennyquick more comfortable, he looked so awkward just lying there. Anyway, wasn't there something about keeping a person warm after an accident?

He had to do *something*.

annotations (margin notes):
- dash and incomplete sentence convey Davy's thoughts
- connective for paragraph
- clues to fear
- tiny details are exaggerated by his shock
- thinking aloud
- new paragraph and use of italics emphasize importance

44

3 Why was he frightened to walk down the pier to get help? *(Rain, wind, waves, dark, slippery, being alone.)*

4 If this adventure happened to you, what would scare you most?

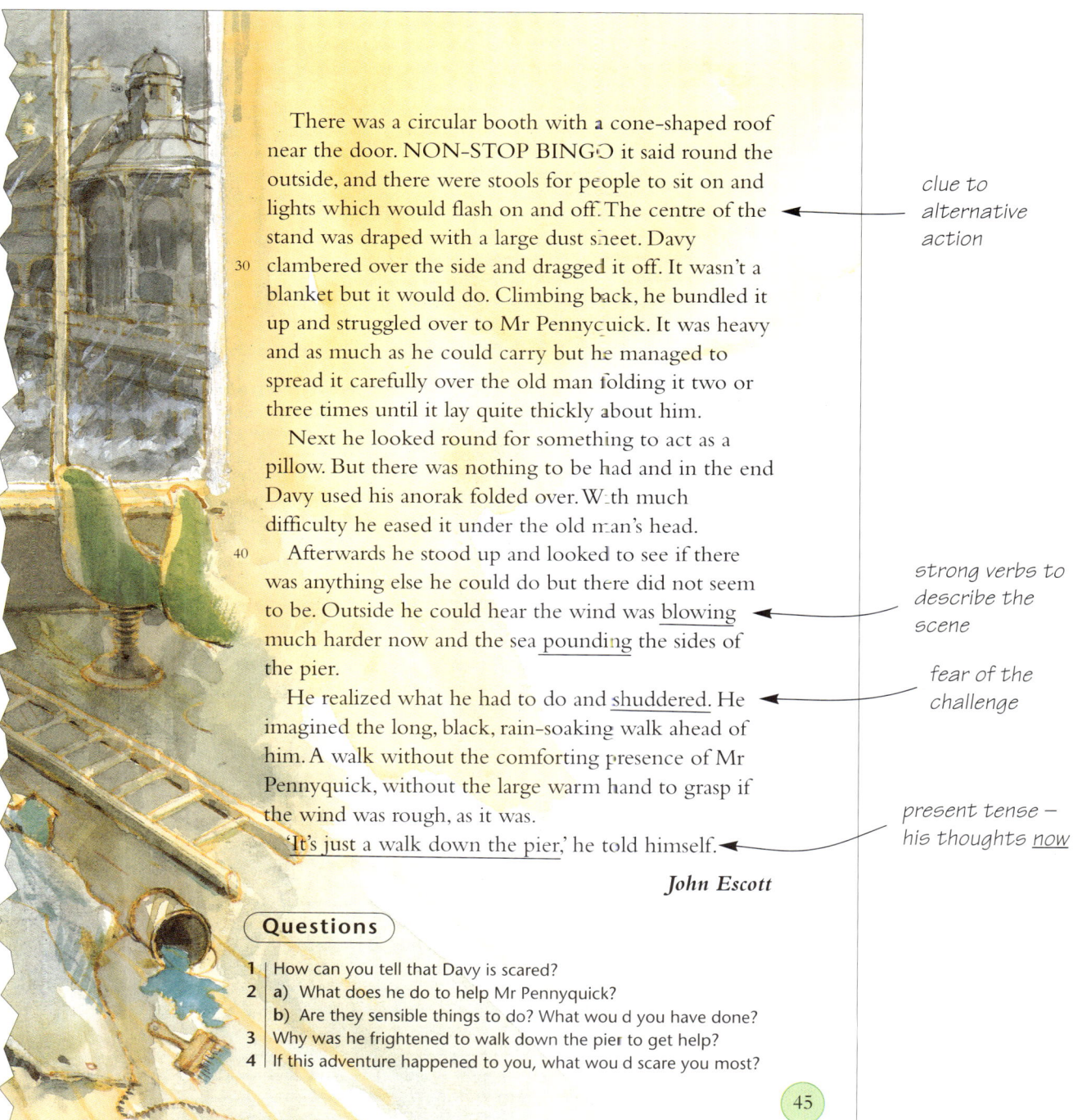

There was a circular booth with a cone-shaped roof near the door. NON-STOP BINGO it said round the outside, and there were stools for people to sit on and lights which would flash on and off. The centre of the stand was draped with a large dust sheet. Davy
30 clambered over the side and dragged it off. It wasn't a blanket but it would do. Climbing back, he bundled it up and struggled over to Mr Pennyquick. It was heavy and as much as he could carry but he managed to spread it carefully over the old man folding it two or three times until it lay quite thickly about him.

Next he looked round for something to act as a pillow. But there was nothing to be had and in the end Davy used his anorak folded over. With much difficulty he eased it under the old man's head.

40 Afterwards he stood up and looked to see if there was anything else he could do but there did not seem to be. Outside he could hear the wind was blowing much harder now and the sea pounding the sides of the pier.

He realized what he had to do and shuddered. He imagined the long, black, rain-soaking walk ahead of him. A walk without the comforting presence of Mr Pennyquick, without the large warm hand to grasp if the wind was rough, as it was.

'It's just a walk down the pier,' he told himself.

John Escott

clue to alternative action

strong verbs to describe the scene

fear of the challenge

present tense – his thoughts now

Questions

1 How can you tell that Davy is scared?
2 a) What does he do to help Mr Pennyquick?
  b) Are they sensible things to do? What would you have done?
3 Why was he frightened to walk down the pier to get help?
4 If this adventure happened to you, what would scare you most?

45

Unit 20 : Whatever the Weather

Main learning objective

● To summarize a sentence or paragraph by identifying the most important elements and rewording them in a limited number of words

Whole class

Introduction

This passage is about the weather. As we read through the passage begin to think about the most important pieces of information.

Read the passage to the children and discuss it with them. Turn to pages 88–9 for the teacher's version of the text and Questions.

Independent work

Activities: Reading

● Reading Skills A (page 21) or B (page 21).
● To be worked on as an independent exercise.

Guided reading/Extension work

1 Read each paragraph and give it a heading.
2 List the key facts from the fourth paragraph. Write these up in simple note form.
3 Decide what illustrations might go well with the fourth paragraph. Think about the main fact/s that could be illustrated.
4 Decide what caption could go with each illustration.

Whole class

Plenary discussion

1 Discuss which sentence in the last paragraph is the most important – and why.
2 What key facts did they find out about the Great Storm? Ask the children using Reading Skills Book A to sum it up in less than ten words (as in their Question 1).

Homework

Collect from home a list of sayings to do with the weather – or any ways in which people predict the weather without listening to the forecast. These could be collected and fed back at the start of the next session.

Additional activities

Sentence and word work

1 Create an index to go with this passage. To do this, find the key words. List them in alphabetical order. There will not be a word for every letter of the alphabet.

2 Create a glossary for the passage. To do this find the more difficult words. Write a simple definition beside each word chosen.

Activities: Writing

● Writing Skills (page 42) — turning a set of notes into three paragraphs of writing, using **Worksheet 25** (Bad Weather).

1. What does the first paragraph tell us? *(Make sure the children re-read the first paragraph. You can sometimes tell the weather from looking at the clouds.)*

2. What is the table about? *(It describes different types of cloud. Many children get lost in the detail. You may need to say 'Is it about different types of rain?')*

alliterative title

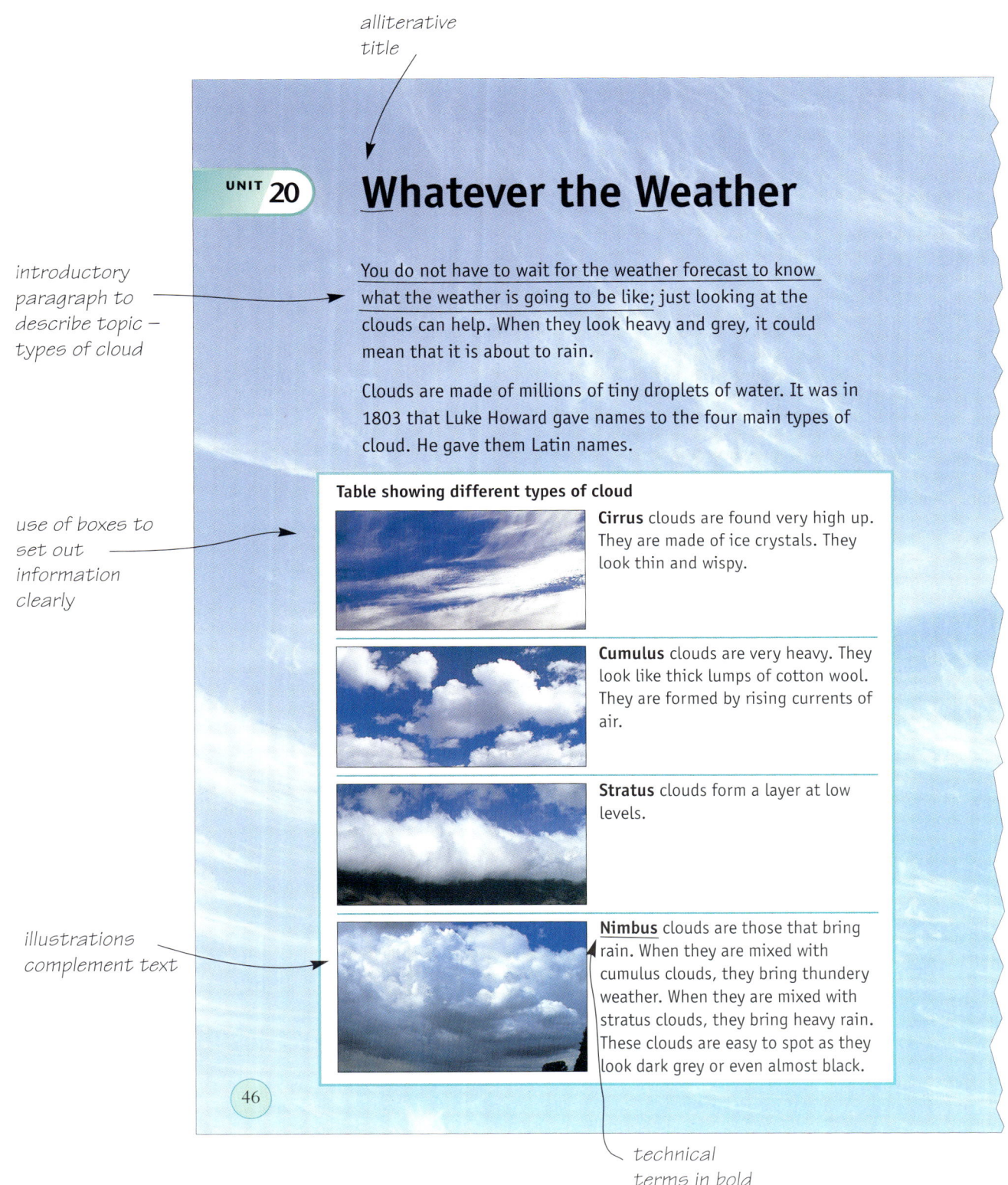

UNIT 20

Whatever the Weather

introductory paragraph to describe topic – types of cloud

You do not have to wait for the weather forecast to know what the weather is going to be like; just looking at the clouds can help. When they look heavy and grey, it could mean that it is about to rain.

Clouds are made of millions of tiny droplets of water. It was in 1803 that Luke Howard gave names to the four main types of cloud. He gave them Latin names.

Table showing different types of cloud

use of boxes to set out information clearly

Cirrus clouds are found very high up. They are made of ice crystals. They look thin and wispy.

Cumulus clouds are very heavy. They look like thick lumps of cotton wool. They are formed by rising currents of air.

Stratus clouds form a layer at low levels.

illustrations complement text

Nimbus clouds are those that bring rain. When they are mixed with cumulus clouds, they bring thundery weather. When they are mixed with stratus clouds, they bring heavy rain. These clouds are easy to spot as they look dark grey or even almost black.

46

technical terms in bold

3 What is the third paragraph about? *(In Britain the weather can change rapidly.)*

4 What facts can you find in the last paragraph but one? *(Weather varies according to the direction of the wind; forecasters can get it wrong; there was a hurricane in 1987, etc.)*

reason why the weather changes rapidly

The weather in Britain can change rapidly. This means that it is quite possible to have snow one day and hot sun on the next. Sometimes, the air from northern Canada blows across the Atlantic Ocean. This is very cold and brings strong winds and rain. Cold air from the Arctic brings snow. In summer, warmer air from the tropics brings hot weather. If the wind blows from the Sahara desert, in Africa, the temperature rises suddenly and we have a heat wave.

Because the wind can blow in different directions we sometimes get very different weather. It is not always easy for weather forecasters to predict accurately what is going to happen. In October 1987 they failed to predict the Great Storm. This was a hurricane which blew down trees, overturned cars and tore roofs off houses all across the south of England.

Whatever the weather, most of us like to have some variety. It is hard to imagine what it is like in countries where the sun shines all day long, almost every day of the year. Many scientists believe that our climate is changing. Over the next hundred years the weather may become hotter. Whilst this may please some people, it would mean that our daily lives would have to change.

weather forecasting is not easy

inverted sentence with conjunction as first word, gives emphasis

Storm damage, October 1987.

looking to the future

Questions

1 | What does the first paragraph tell us?
2 | What is the second paragraph about?
3 | What is the third paragraph about?
4 | What facts can you find in the last paragraph but one?

47

Unit 21 : Why?

Main learning objectives

- To understand the theme and mood of a poem
- To recognize some simple forms of poetry – the question/list poem
- To look at how a poet does or does not use rhyme

Read the poem to the children and discuss it with them. Turn to pages 92–3 for the teacher's version of the text and Questions.

Whole class

Introduction

Many poems are about things that poets are unsure about. Sometimes they are expressed in questions. This poem poses a number of questions.

Read the poem to the children and discuss it with them. Turn to pages 92–3 for the teacher's version of the text and Questions.

Hi! I'm orange!

Independent work

Activities: Reading

- Reading Skills A (page 22) or B (page 22).
- To be worked on as an independent exercise.

And I'm yellow!

Guided reading/Extension work

1 Take a verse and re-write it as dialogue, giving the reply made by an adult or another child. Repeat with other verses.
2 Ask everyone in the group to write an additional question. Check that each person uses a question mark. If someone gets stuck on a spelling, discuss spelling strategies (spelling rules, saying a word slowly and writing down the sounds, breaking a word into syllables, using analogy, building from known words or parts of words, writing the word down and looking at it, etc.)

Just call me red!

Whole class

Plenary discussion

Ask the children to share their views on:

- the mood of the poem
- what makes this a poem rather than a list of sentences. *(Both questions are in the Skills books.)* Does a poem have to rhyme?

Homework

Use **Worksheet 26** (Editing a Poem). Read the worksheet and make the poem more effective by crossing out unnecessary words.

Additional activities

Sentence and word work

1 Take some of the verses and change them into statements, using speech marks, e.g. 'Why does my mum always iron a crease in my jeans?' becomes 'My mum always irons a crease in my jeans.'

2 Revisit 'wh' words and list them as a reminder. Think of ways to remember correct spellings, e.g. there is a 'hen' in 'when', a 'hat' in 'what'.

Activities: Writing

- Writing Skills (page 44) – writing a question and answer poem in pairs.

- Shared writing (teacher-led) is followed by an independent task.

1 What is the effect of not using rhyme? (Compare this poem with 'Wish Wish Wish' on pages 26–7.) *(Most children will say that the 'wish' poem sounds like a poem but this one is more like a list of sentences. This poem does not use rhyme and has no obvious rhythm.)*

2 What is the mood or feeling of the poem? *(Various: questioning, obviously – some may suggest that the poet is complaining. There are questions in the Skills books which explore this area further.)*

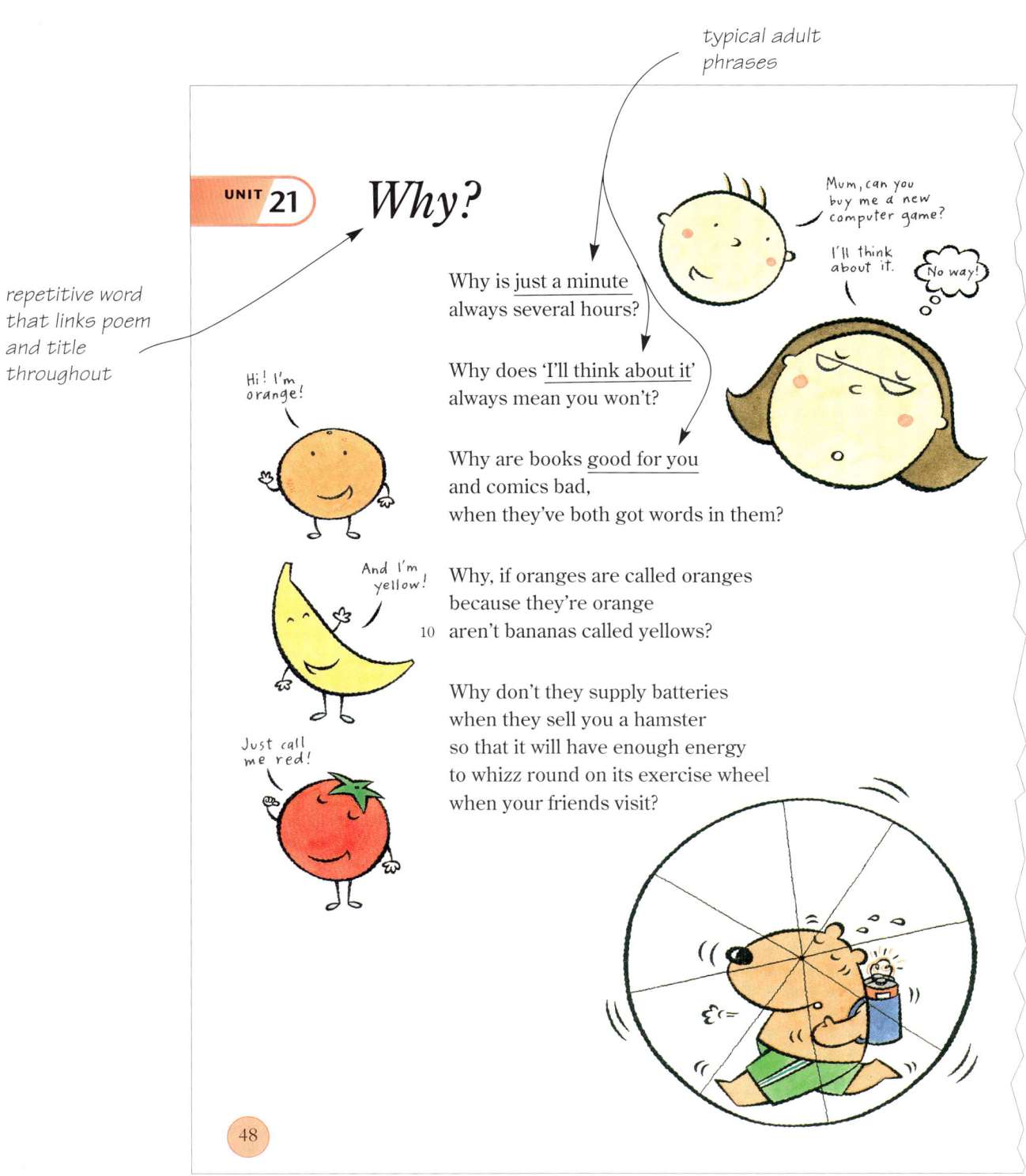

typical adult phrases

repetitive word that links poem and title throughout

UNIT **21**

Why?

Hi! I'm orange!

And I'm yellow!

Just call me red!

Mum, can you buy me a new computer game?

I'll think about it.

No way!

Why is just a minute
always several hours?

Why does 'I'll think about it'
always mean you won't?

Why are books good for you
and comics bad,
when they've both got words in them?

Why, if oranges are called oranges
because they're orange
10 aren't bananas called yellows?

Why don't they supply batteries
when they sell you a hamster
so that it will have enough energy
to whizz round on its exercise wheel
when your friends visit?

48

Are there any questions that you often ask?
(Various possible answers. They may need a minute to discuss it with a partner.)

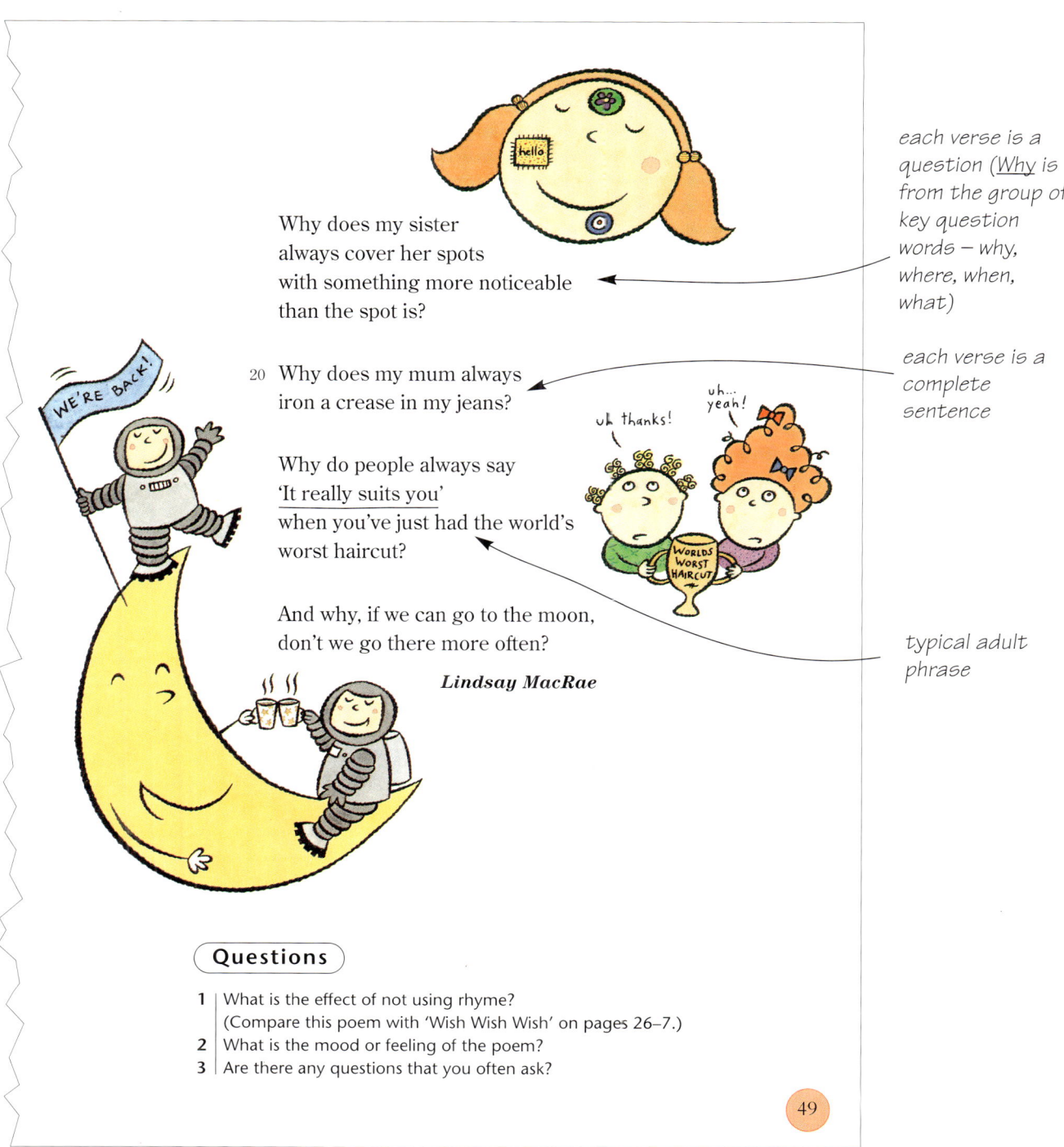

Why does my sister
always cover her spots
with something more noticeable
than the spot is?

each verse is a question (<u>Why</u> is from the group of key question words – why, where, when, what)

20 Why does my mum always
iron a crease in my jeans?

each verse is a complete sentence

Why do people always say
'It really suits <u>you</u>'
when you've just had the world's
worst haircut?

typical adult phrase

And why, if we can go to the moon,
don't we go there more often?

Lindsay MacRae

uh thanks!

uh... yeah!

WORLDS WORST HAIRCUT

WE'RE BACK!

hello

(**Questions**)

1 | What is the effect of not using rhyme?
    (Compare this poem with 'Wish Wish Wish' on pages 26–7.)
2 | What is the mood or feeling of the poem?
3 | Are there any questions that you often ask?

49

Unit 22 : Dick King-Smith

Main learning objective

- To make comparisons and identify familiar features in a writer's work

Whole class

Introduction

We are going to read some short extracts from different stories by the same author and look for things that they have in common.

All Dick King-Smith's stories have animals in them. Perhaps the most famous one is 'The Sheep-Pig' which was made into the film, 'Babe'. In the three extracts here, we meet a parrot, a family of hedgehogs, a dog and a cat.

In 'Harry's Mad', Harry's great uncle George leaves him Madison the parrot in his will. Madison turns out to be rather unusual.

Read the extract to the children and discuss it with them. Turn to page 96 for the teacher's version of the text and Questions.

In 'The Hodgeheg', Max the hedgehog tries to cross the road at a zebra crossing, but he finds out that lorries only stop for people, not hedgehogs. Luckily he isn't killed, but he gets a bad bump on the head.

Read the extract to the children and discuss it with them. Turn to page 97 for the teacher's version of the text and Questions.

'Find the White Horse' is a story about a dog who escapes from a dogs' home, helped by his friend Squintum, the Siamese cat. Lubber isn't very clever, and Squintum has to explain to him what danger he is in.

Read the extract to the children and discuss it with them. Turn to pages 98–9 for the teacher's version of the text and Questions.

Independent work

Activities: Reading

- Reading Skills A (page 23) or B (page 23).
- The children will need **Worksheet 28** (Missing Words and Phrases).
- To be worked on as an independent exercise.

Guided reading/Extension work

1 Re-read the third extract, taking turns with parts and reading in character. Think about words such as 'muttered' and 'said slowly' and read the extract accordingly. How will Lubber sound in his first speech? *(Unsure, hesitating.)* Note the effect of the dashes and the question at the end. And how will Squintum sound? Why does Lubber say his last speech slowly?

2 Re-word the question 'Humans don't kill dogs, surely?' as a definite statement 'Humans don't kill dogs.' Point out that it is a kind of half-question. 'Do humans kill dogs?' would be a more direct question – why doesn't Lubber say it like that?

3 Read the first extract in the same way. How can you tell that Madison is American? Try an American accent!

4 Look at Max's muddled words in the second extract. Invent some more! Try changing nouns and verbs as in 'headed my bang', e.g. 'I balled the kick'.

Whole class

Plenary discussion

List some of the good things about the animals and the bad things about humans. Share favourite funny bits.

Homework

Use **Worksheet 27** (Muddled Words) to translate some muddled words and phrases.

Additional activities

Sentence and word work

1 Changing sentence types (third extract): change 'Are you hurt?' into a statement. Then turn Lubber's statements into questions, e.g. 'You said those humans were going to kill me.' Note the changes in word order.

2 Words with common roots (first extract): think about the word 'telephone'. Look at other words with 'tele' or 'phone' in them, e.g. television, telescope, microphone, phoneme. Use a dictionary to find out the meaning of 'tele' and 'phone', from the Greek *('distant/ sound')*. What does 'television' mean?

3 Look at the spelling of 'shun' endings. Start with 'expression', in the third extract, line 18. Ask the children for other 'shun' words. Make lists which can be added to over time, and learned.

4 Revise the use of speech marks. Point out that speech marks round titles separate them from the rest of the sentence.

Activities: Writing

● Writing Skills (page 46) – planning a presentation on a favourite author.

● Shared writing (teacher-led) is followed by an independent task.

1 What things do these three extracts have in common? *(Animals that talk and behave like humans, humans that don't seem to understand animals, humour.)*

2 Why do Madison's claws tighten on Harry's shoulder? *(He's anxious. He does not want Harry to tell his friends because it will lead to trouble.)*

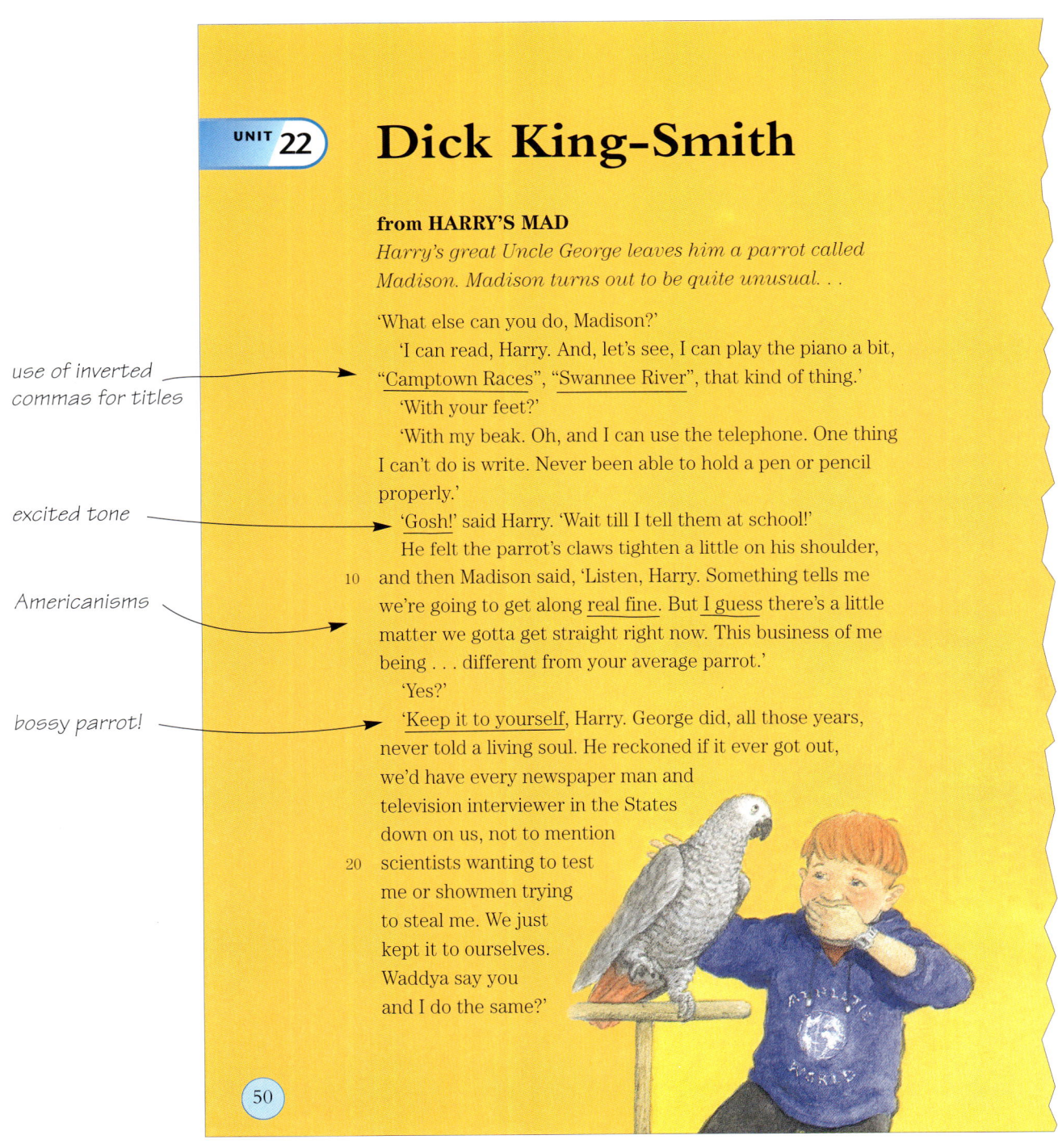

UNIT **22**

Dick King-Smith

from HARRY'S MAD

Harry's great Uncle George leaves him a parrot called Madison. Madison turns out to be quite unusual...

'What else can you do, Madison?'

'I can read, Harry. And, let's see, I can play the piano a bit, "Camptown Races", "Swannee River", that kind of thing.'

use of inverted commas for titles

'With your feet?'

'With my beak. Oh, and I can use the telephone. One thing I can't do is write. Never been able to hold a pen or pencil properly.'

'Gosh!' said Harry. 'Wait till I tell them at school!'

excited tone

He felt the parrot's claws tighten a little on his shoulder,
10 and then Madison said, 'Listen, Harry. Something tells me we're going to get along real fine. But I guess there's a little

Americanisms

matter we gotta get straight right now. This business of me being . . . different from your average parrot.'

'Yes?'

'Keep it to yourself, Harry. George did, all those years,

bossy parrot!

never told a living soul. He reckoned if it ever got out, we'd have every newspaper man and television interviewer in the States down on us, not to mention
20 scientists wanting to test me or showmen trying to steal me. We just kept it to ourselves. Waddya say you and I do the same?'

50

3 Why does Max get his words muddled up?
(He has concussion.)

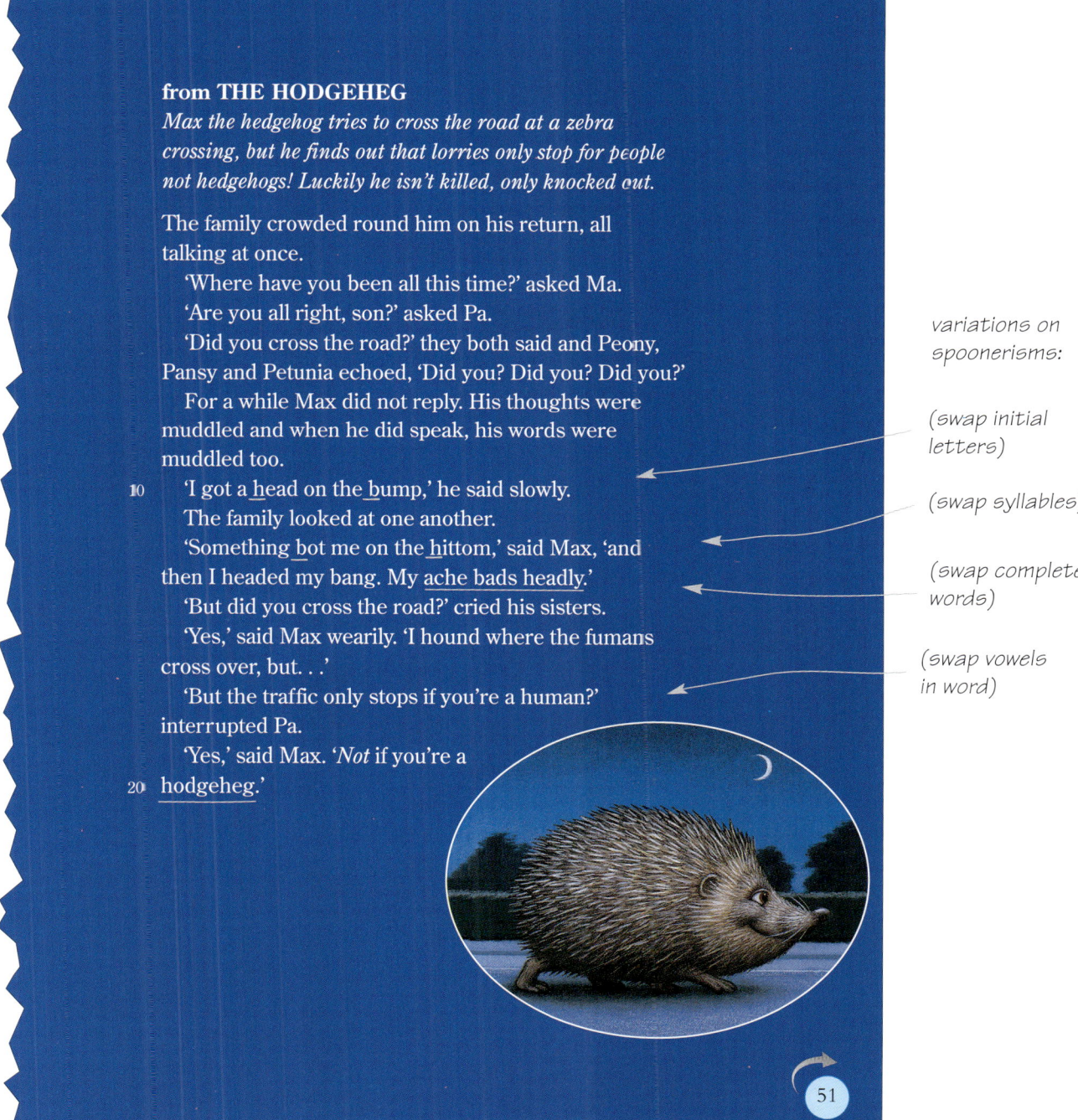

from THE HODGEHEG

Max the hedgehog tries to cross the road at a zebra crossing, but he finds out that lorries only stop for people not hedgehogs! Luckily he isn't killed, only knocked out.

The family crowded round him on his return, all talking at once.

'Where have you been all this time?' asked Ma.

'Are you all right, son?' asked Pa.

'Did you cross the road?' they both said and Peony, Pansy and Petunia echoed, 'Did you? Did you? Did you?'

For a while Max did not reply. His thoughts were muddled and when he did speak, his words were muddled too.

10 'I got a head on the bump,' he said slowly.

The family looked at one another.

'Something bot me on the hittom,' said Max, 'and then I headed my bang. My ache bads headly.'

'But did you cross the road?' cried his sisters.

'Yes,' said Max wearily. 'I hound where the fumans cross over, but. . .'

'But the traffic only stops if you're a human?' interrupted Pa.

'Yes,' said Max. '*Not* if you're a

20 hodgeheg.'

variations on spoonerisms:

(swap initial letters)

(swap syllables)

(swap complete words)

(swap vowels in word)

51

4 How can you tell that Lubber doesn't understand what danger he's in? *(He says he likes going to sleep.)*

5 Which story do you like best? Why? Take a vote.

from FIND THE WHITE HORSE
This is a story about a dog called Lubber who escapes from a dog's home helped by his friend, Squintum the Siamese cat. Lubber isn't very clever and Squintum has to explain what danger he is in.

Lubber isn't very bright

'I don't understand,' he muttered. 'You said those humans were going to kill me. But humans aren't like that, Squintum. I've never seen that man in the white coat before, but that girl – she was kind to me while I was in that place. And my own people at home – where I've always lived, before I got lost, that is – they've always been ever so good to me. Humans don't kill

disbelief

dogs, surely?'

52

UNIT 22 ● Dick King-Smith

'Sometimes they do,' said Squintum, and he
10 explained everything about the Dogs' Home and places
like it, and why, because people are either <u>thoughtless</u>
<u>or cruel</u>, there are so many stray dogs abandoned by
their owners.

'Too many to cope with,' he finished, 'so they just
put them to sleep.'

'But I don't mind <u>going to sleep</u>,' said Lubber. 'In
fact, I love it.'

'It's an expression,' said Squintum. 'They kill them.
They were about to <u>kill you</u>. I saved you.'

'Oh,' said Lubber slowly. 'Oh, how can I ever thank
you enough?'

*unkind/bad
humans
contrasted with
good/innocent
animals*

*firmly telling the
truth*

*slowly dawning on
him*

**Dick King-Smith,
who wrote these
three stories and
many more.**

(**Questions**)

1 | What things do these three extracts have in common?
2 | Why do Madison's claws tighten on Harry's shoulder?
3 | Why does Max get his words muddled up?
4 | How can you tell that Lubber doesn't understand what
danger he's in?
5 | Which story do you like best? Why? Take a vote.

53

Unit 23 : Recipe for a Class Outing

Main learning objectives

- To read and understand a poem that capitalizes upon another text type to create humour
- To identify features of instructional writing

Whole class

Introduction

This poem is unusual. It has been written in the form of a different type of writing.

Read the poem to the children and discuss it with them. Turn to pages 102–103 for the teacher's version of the text and Questions.

Independent work

Activities: Reading

- Reading Skills A (page 24) or B (page 24).
- To be worked on as an independent exercise.

Guided reading/Extension work

1 Re-read the 'method' section. Invent other possible lines for the poem. Use typical 'recipe' words to start the sentences, such as: add, stir, leave, place in the oven, sprinkle, add a pinch, beat, cover, place, boil, put.

2 Revisit the work on instructional texts in Unit 16 ('Hot Air Balloons'), and think about whether this recipe has all the structural elements – an introduction, materials or ingredients, method in logical order, concluding statement.

3 Write an introductory section for the recipe, in the correct style, e.g. This recipe is ideal for a hot summery day, but it needs careful cooking or it can boil over.

Whole class

Plenary discussion

Talk about whether this is a poem or an imaginative recipe.

Homework

Write a conversation between one of the teachers and the headteacher when they got back. Begin with the headteacher asking how the trip went. What would the teacher say?

Sentence and word work

1   Re-read the 'method' section. Identify the verbs and add possible adverbs. Use the correct terminology and encourage the children to do so. Try different adverbs to gain different effects. Discuss how the adverb tells the reader more about the verb. What happens to the meaning if, after the verb, 'heat', you add 'fast' or 'slowly'?

2   Ask the children to spot the common spelling pattern in the adverbs. Then list other adverbs which share a common spelling pattern.

3   Use a dictionary to find out what 'season', 'simmer' and 'garnish' mean.

Activities: Writing

● Writing Skills (page 48) – writing a recipe poem for a party using Sue Cowling's poem as a model.

● Shared writing (teacher-led) is followed by an independent task using **Worksheet 29** (Recipe Words and Phrases).

1) Which ingredients tell you that the class outing was not a great success? *(The nosebleed, fights, lost purses and torn dress. Of course, a hot day does not necessarily spoil an outing and neither does singing.)*

2) Find two clues that show what time of year it was. *(Clues such as 'hot day' and 'heat slowly' tell us that it is probably a summer trip.)*

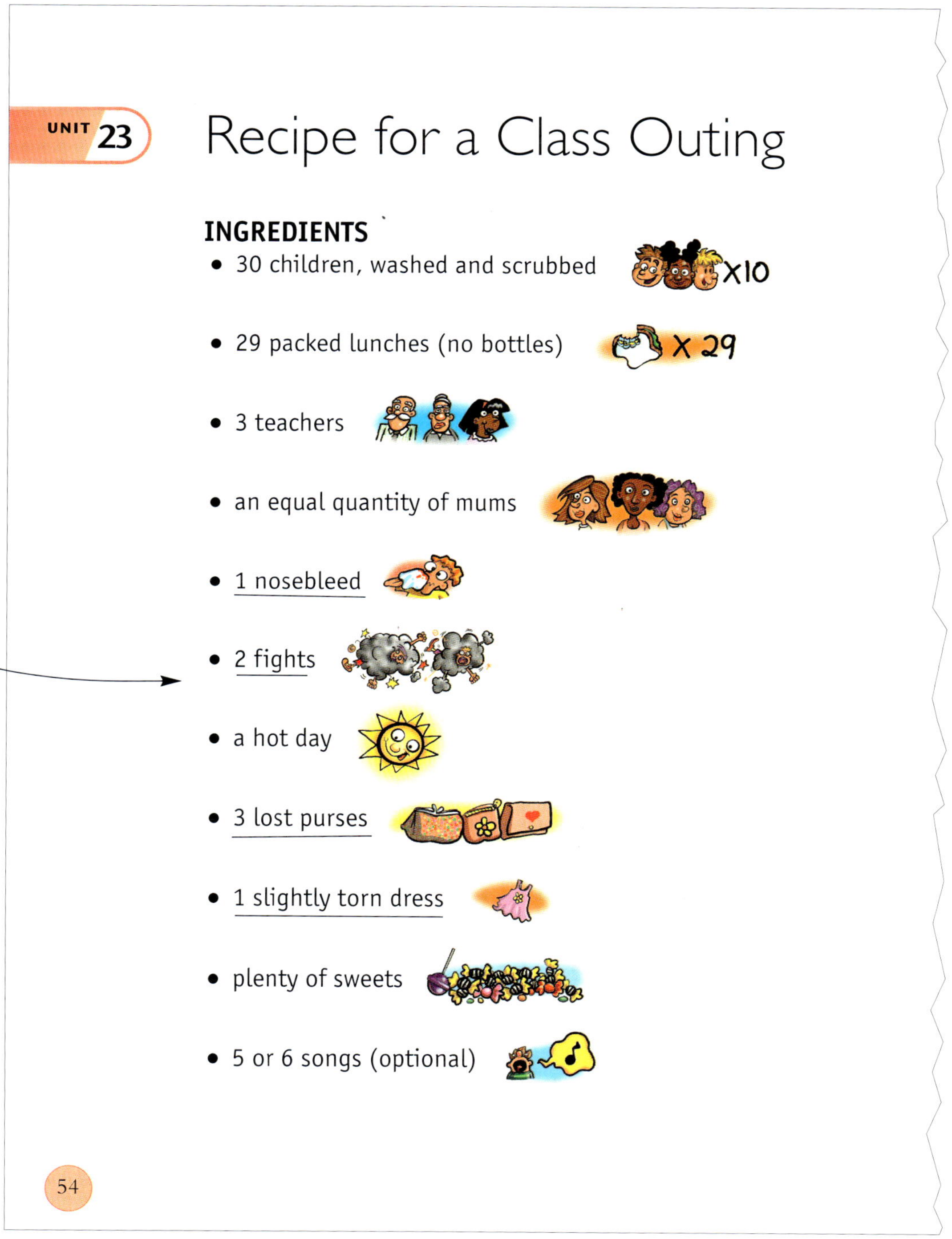

UNIT 23

Recipe for a Class Outing

INGREDIENTS

- 30 children, washed and scrubbed x10

- 29 packed lunches (no bottles) X 29

- 3 teachers

- an equal quantity of mums

- 1 nosebleed

ingredients that spell trouble

- 2 fights

- a hot day

- 3 lost purses

- 1 slightly torn dress

- plenty of sweets

- 5 or 6 songs (optional)

54

3 Find three phrases or words that come from a recipe. *(Any of the following: ingredients, place, heat slowly, season well, heat to boiling point, add, simmer, remove, leave to cool, stir in, return to heat, mix thoroughly, drain, divide into individual portions, serve, garnish.)*

4 Look at the 'method' section. Where in the sentences are most of the verbs? *(Most of the verbs are at the start of the sentences – in the imperative form – they are like 'commands'.)*

METHOD

<u>Place</u> children and adults in a bus and heat slowly.

<u>Season well</u> with sweets, reserving a few for later. ← *Instructions use imperative mood. Verbs come first.*

<u>Heat</u> to boiling point. Add fights and nosebleed.

Leave to simmer for 2 hours.

Remove children and packed lunches and leave to cool.

<u>Stir in</u> torn dress and lost purses.

Return to heat, <u>add</u> songs <u>to taste</u>.

Mix thoroughly. If the children go soggy and start to
    stick together, remove from bus and drain.

At the end of the cooking time <u>divide into individual</u> ← *typical recipe terms*
    <u>portions</u> (makes about 36).

Serve with relief, <u>garnished</u> liberally with dirt.

Sue Cowling

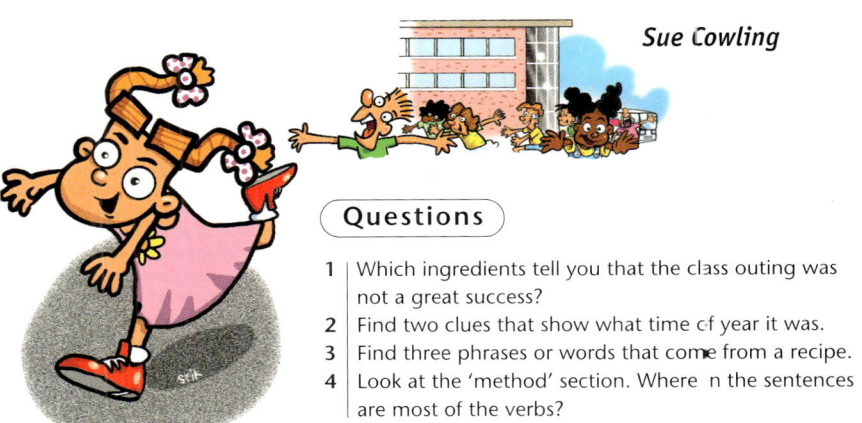

Questions

1 | Which ingredients tell you that the class outing was not a great success?
2 | Find two clues that show what time of year it was.
3 | Find three phrases or words that come from a recipe.
4 | Look at the 'method' section. Where n the sentences are most of the verbs?

55

Unit 24 : The Fallen Elephant

Main learning objectives

● To focus on differences in place, etc.

● To identify social, moral or cultural issues in stories

Whole class

Introduction

Imagine living in the heart of Africa. Imagine living in a place where the sun rises each morning over blue mountains, and great plains where the grass grows taller than a man. Imagine living in a place where there are still elephants. Akimbo lives in such a place, on the edge of a game reserve where animals can live in safety. His father is a game warden. He has to try to protect the elephants from poachers who want to steal the elephants' ivory tusks.

Read the extract to the children and discuss it with them. Turn to pages 106–108 for the teacher's version of the text and Questions.

Independent work

Activities: Reading

● Reading Skills A (page 25) or B (page 25).

● To be worked on as an independent exercise.

Guided reading/Extension work

1 Look at the change of tense (lines 35–7). Why is that sentence in the present tense? Explain that it's not part of the story, it's giving us information – facts about what African animals do.

2 Read lines 40–43. Why is there a new paragraph? Why did the man suddenly hit the truck roof? Point out how that bit of the story is suddenly urgent – you know something important is going to happen. And then you start dreading what it might be, just like the characters in the story. Jump on to look at line 62 'secretly dreading'. And then there's a bigger break than a paragraph – there's a gap as well. Why is it there?

3 Read lines 13–34 with the children taking the parts of Akimbo and his father. The speech from lines 16–21 should be divided up. Point out the conventions for speech marks and new paragraphs. How could you make lines 28–34 more interesting? Which are the most important words which tell us what it must have felt like? Look at 'scrape', 'painful', 'jarring' and 'wince'. Try replacing those words with words which are less powerful. Notice what is lost.

Whole class

Plenary discussion

Ask the children to read their poems and notes about Akimbo's feelings. Suggest that the children working on Reading Skills Book A use their notes in a future Writing Task session to write a poem.

Discuss further why elephants are killed for their ivory and why it is wrong.

Homework

Make notes about African elephants and ivory from **Worksheet 30** (Elephant Fact Sheet). Find out any more information you can.

Or

Use **Worksheet 31** (Apostrophes) to put apostrophes in the right places, and to write out contracted words in full.

Additional activities

Sentence and word work

1 Apostrophes: distinguish between contractions (it'll, isn't) and possessive (Akimbo's father, the man's gaze). Ask the children which letters are missing from the contractions and write the words in full. Then look at 'the elephant lay on its side' – there is no apostrophe.

2 Adding prefixes and suffixes: look at 'eager*ly*', 'unmerciful*ly*', 'unbearab*ly*', 'pain*ful*'. Break the words down into their main part (stem) and their prefix or suffix. Decide whether the main part is a noun, adjective or verb 'eager', 'mercy',' bear', 'pain'. Look at the prefixes and suffixes 'un', 'ly', 'able', 'ably', 'ful', 'fully'. Try the suffixes with other words, e.g. 'quiet', 'wash', 'comfort', 'kind'. Which ones work? What do the different prefixes and suffixes mean?

3 Compound words: 'undergrowth', 'pothole', 'waterhole'. What do the words mean? Look at how it helps spelling and meaning to think about the separate parts. Think of other compound words and their meanings and spellings, e.g. 'handbag', 'bedroom', 'classroom' and 'football'.

Activities: Writing

- Writing Skills (page 50) – making a poster to help the elephants.
- Shared writing (teacher-led) is followed by an independent task, continuing with the design of the poster.

Questions

1 What is the first sign that something is wrong? *(Vultures.)*

2 What makes them think that the vultures aren't finishing off a lion's meal? *(There are so many vultures, it must be a very big animal – Akimbo starts to guess what it might be.)*

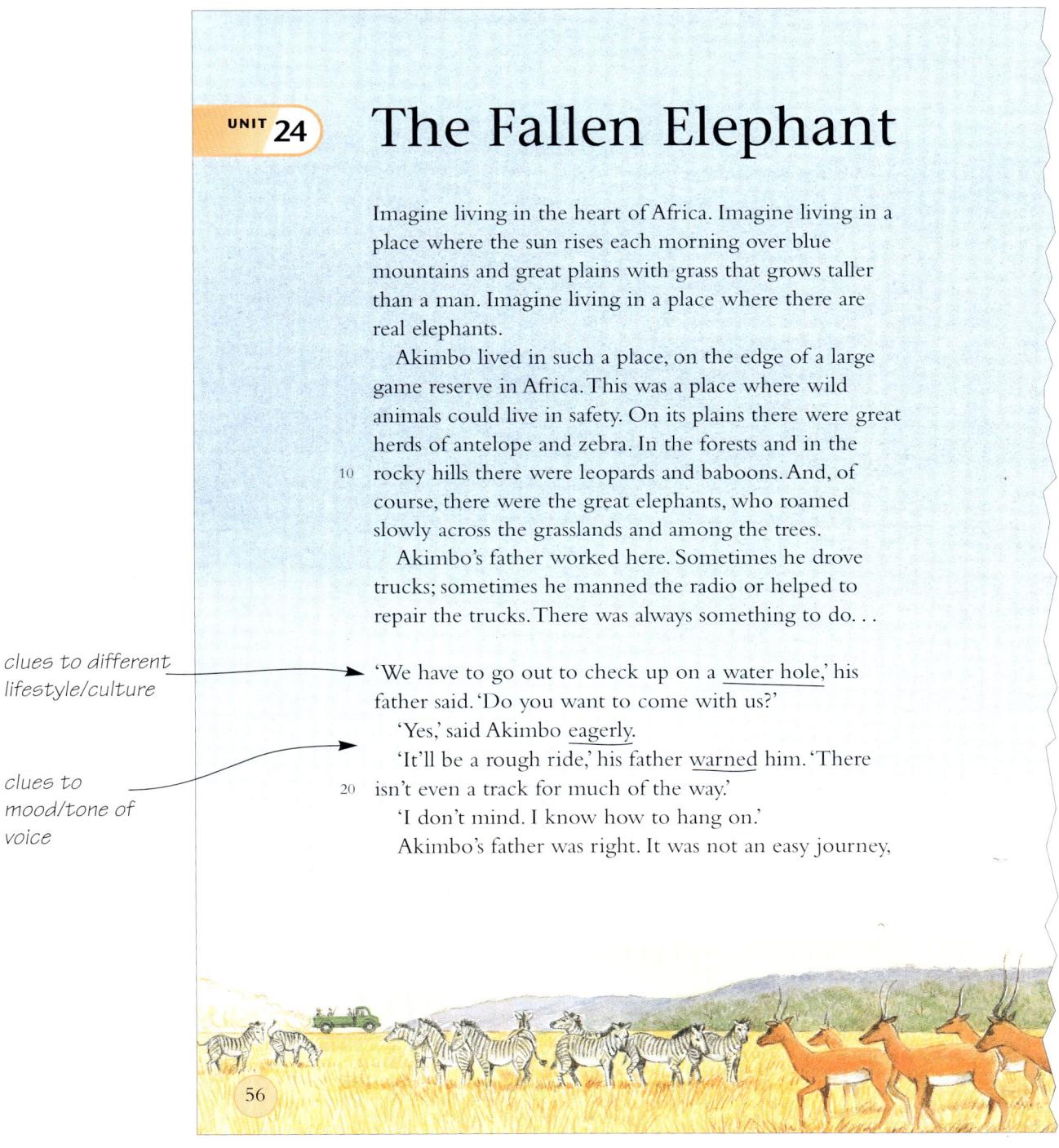

UNIT **24**

The Fallen Elephant

Imagine living in the heart of Africa. Imagine living in a place where the sun rises each morning over blue mountains and great plains with grass that grows taller than a man. Imagine living in a place where there are real elephants.

Akimbo lived in such a place, on the edge of a large game reserve in Africa. This was a place where wild animals could live in safety. On its plains there were great herds of antelope and zebra. In the forests and in the
10 rocky hills there were leopards and baboons. And, of course, there were the great elephants, who roamed slowly across the grasslands and among the trees.

Akimbo's father worked here. Sometimes he drove trucks; sometimes he manned the radio or helped to repair the trucks. There was always something to do. . .

clues to different lifestyle/culture

'We have to go out to check up on a water hole,' his father said. 'Do you want to come with us?'

'Yes,' said Akimbo eagerly.

clues to mood/tone of voice

'It'll be a rough ride,' his father warned him. 'There
20 isn't even a track for much of the way.'

'I don't mind. I know how to hang on.'

Akimbo's father was right. It was not an easy journey,

56

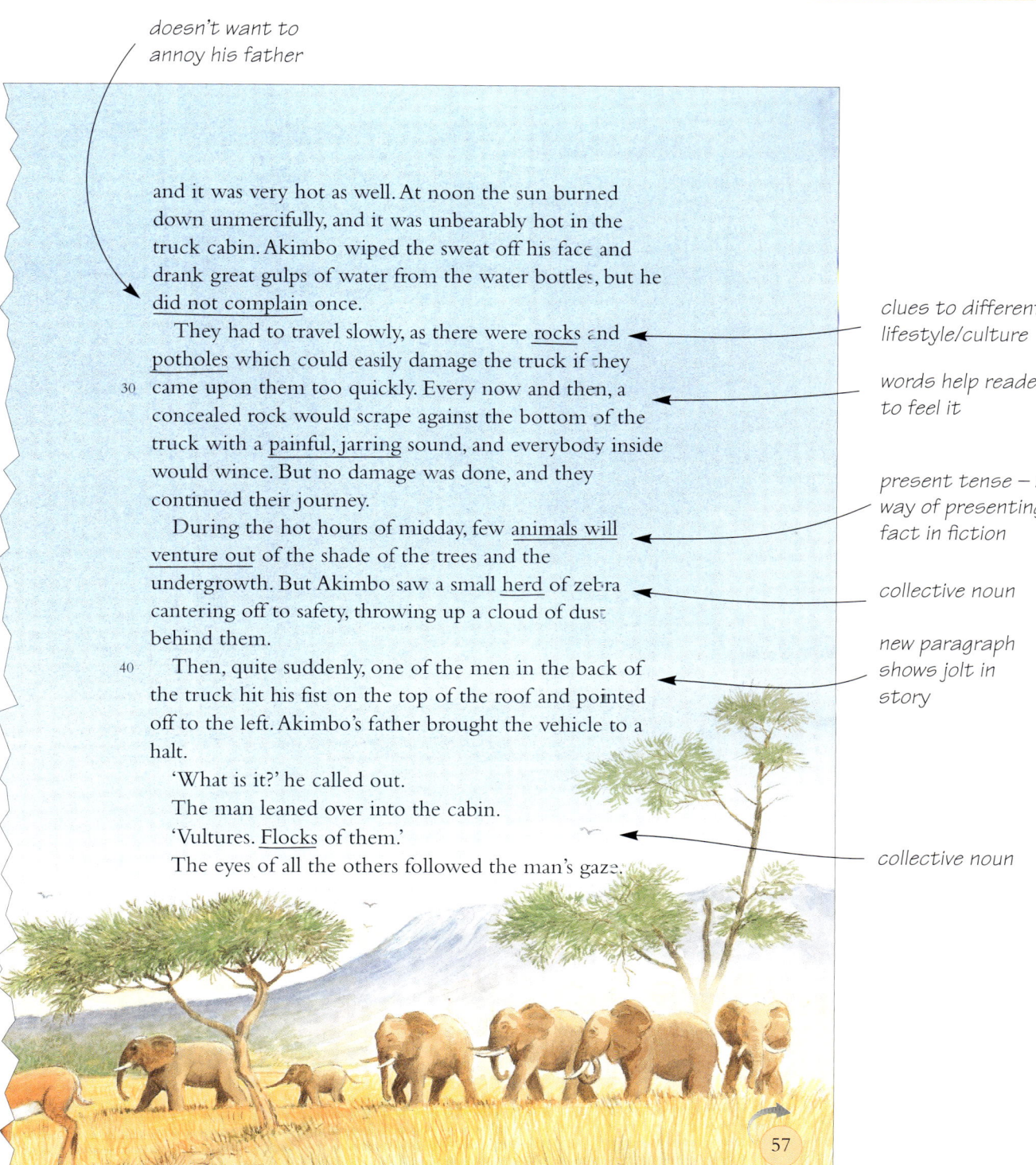

doesn't want to annoy his father

and it was very hot as well. At noon the sun burned down unmercifully, and it was unbearably hot in the truck cabin. Akimbo wiped the sweat off his face and drank great gulps of water from the water bottles, but he did not complain once.

They had to travel slowly, as there were rocks and potholes which could easily damage the truck if they
30 came upon them too quickly. Every now and then, a concealed rock would scrape against the bottom of the truck with a painful, jarring sound, and everybody inside would wince. But no damage was done, and they continued their journey.

During the hot hours of midday, few animals will venture out of the shade of the trees and the undergrowth. But Akimbo saw a small herd of zebra cantering off to safety, throwing up a cloud of dust behind them.

40 Then, quite suddenly, one of the men in the back of the truck hit his fist on the top of the roof and pointed off to the left. Akimbo's father brought the vehicle to a halt.

'What is it?' he called out.

The man leaned over into the cabin.

'Vultures. Flocks of them.'

The eyes of all the others followed the man's gaze.

clues to different lifestyle/culture

words help reader to feel it

present tense – a way of presenting fact in fiction

collective noun

new paragraph shows jolt in story

collective noun

57

UNIT 24 ● The Fallen Elephant   107

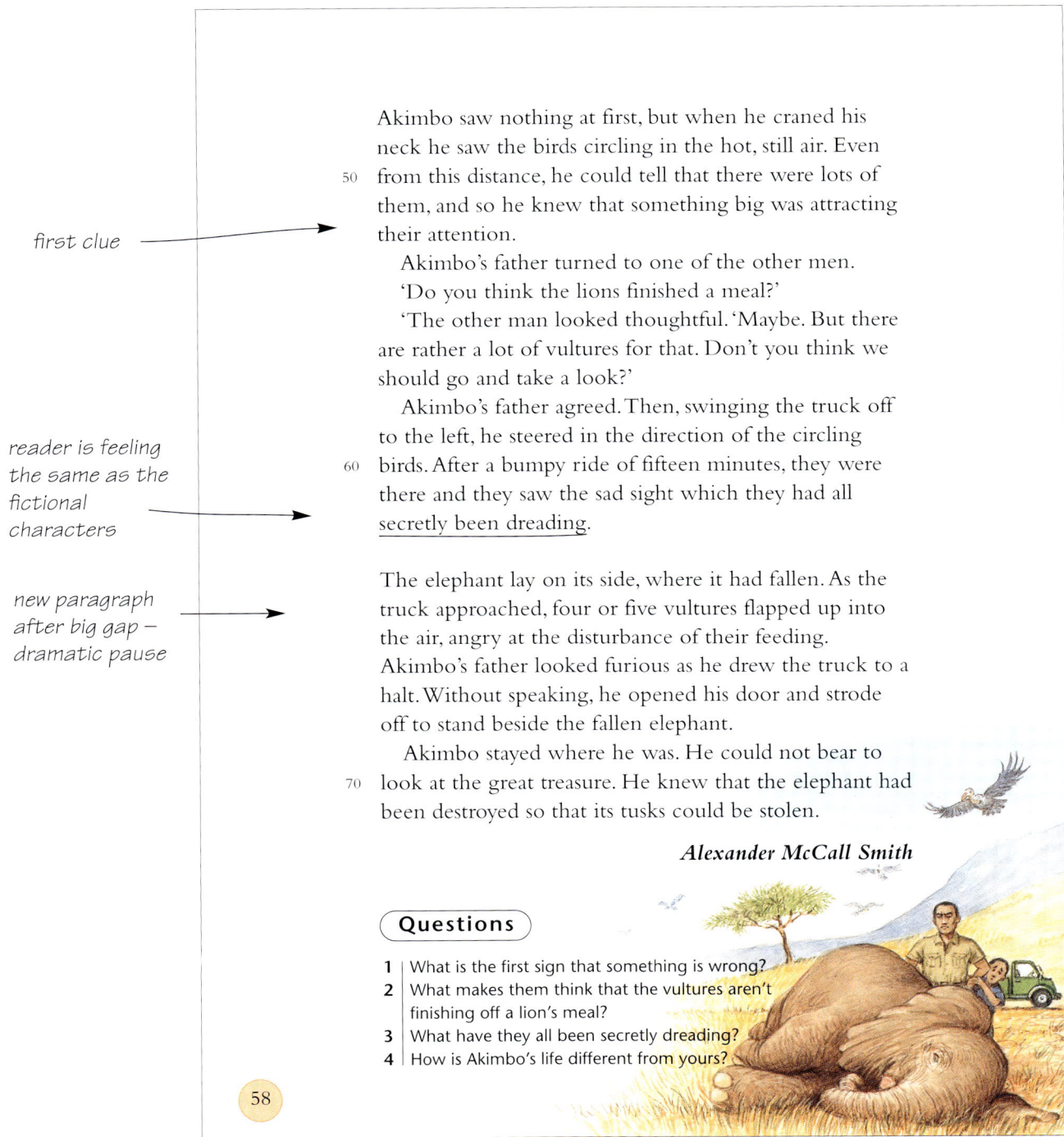

Akimbo saw nothing at first, but when he craned his neck he saw the birds circling in the hot, still air. Even from this distance, he could tell that there were lots of them, and so he knew that something big was attracting their attention.

first clue

Akimbo's father turned to one of the other men.

'Do you think the lions finished a meal?'

'The other man looked thoughtful. 'Maybe. But there are rather a lot of vultures for that. Don't you think we should go and take a look?'

Akimbo's father agreed. Then, swinging the truck off to the left, he steered in the direction of the circling birds. After a bumpy ride of fifteen minutes, they were there and they saw the sad sight which they had all secretly been dreading.

reader is feeling the same as the fictional characters

new paragraph after big gap – dramatic pause

The elephant lay on its side, where it had fallen. As the truck approached, four or five vultures flapped up into the air, angry at the disturbance of their feeding. Akimbo's father looked furious as he drew the truck to a halt. Without speaking, he opened his door and strode off to stand beside the fallen elephant.

Akimbo stayed where he was. He could not bear to look at the great treasure. He knew that the elephant had been destroyed so that its tusks could be stolen.

Alexander McCall Smith

Questions

1 | What is the first sign that something is wrong?
2 | What makes them think that the vultures aren't finishing off a lion's meal?
3 | What have they all been secretly dreading?
4 | How is Akimbo's life different from yours?

58

UNIT 24 ● The Fallen Elephant

Unit 25 : The Door

Main learning objectives

- To read and understand a poem from a different culture set in an imagined world
- To identify a simple pattern in a poem
- To read aloud effectively

Whole class

Introduction

This poem was written by Miroslav Holub, a poet from the Czech Republic. Holub is also a scientist.

Read the poem to the children and discuss it with them. Make sure that they understand the word 'draught'. Turn to page 111 for the teacher's version of the text and Questions.

Independent work

Activities: Reading

- Reading Skills A (page 26) or B (page 26).
- To be worked on in pairs.

Guided reading/Extension work

1 Discuss: if this was a real door, which things might be on the other side? If it is an imaginary door, which things might be on the other side? Which is better – reality or the poet's imagination?

2 Discuss: which lines are the most important and why?

3 Why has the poet used very few adjectives?

Whole class

Plenary discussion

Listen to some of the paired readings. Discuss with the class what is effective about the readings and what areas could be improved.

If there is time, give the class the opportunity to discuss each reading in pairs, using **Worksheet 21** (Evaluation Sheet) and then to feed back comments. Let the performers make their own evaluative comments – 'How we could have done it better?'. Provide further time during the week for the pairs to practise their readings, and listen to their more polished performances towards the end of the week. Encourage variation in volume, pace and the use of movement and sound effects.

Homework

Use **Worksheet 32** (A Muddled Poem). Cut up the lines. Then put the lines back together to make a poem which makes sense. Point out that there is no single correct answer.

Additional activities

Sentence and word work

1 Pick out the nouns that have no adjectives. Write them on the board. As a shared writing activity, add possible adjectives to them.

2 Re-read the poem aloud, inserting the adjectives. How does this affect the picture that the reader sees?

Activities: Writing

● Writing Skills (page 52) – writing a poem that uses the same format as 'The Door'.

● Shared writing (teacher-led) is followed by an independent task.

Questions

1 Which idea do you like best? *(Refer the children back to the text. Why do they like that idea – What does it remind them of? Do they like the sound? Is it the way the words go together? etc.)*

2 Find two adjectives. *('Magic' and 'hollow'. There aren't many adjectives.)*

3 **a)** Which words are repeated? *('Go and open the door, . . . 'maybe', etc)*

b) What effect does this have? *(Various responses – at this stage accept most ideas, such as: it gives the poem a sense of rhythm, it keeps on telling you what to do, etc.)*

4 What does the poet mean by 'darkness ticking'? *(It sounds 'spooky', it is like something in a horror film, or even the sound of a clock ticking at night.)*

UNIT 25 The Door

Go and open the door. ← repeated phrase
  Maybe outside there's
  a tree, or a wood,
  a garden, ← lively images
  or a magic city.

Go and open the door.
  Maybe a dog's rummaging. ← powerful verb
  Maybe you'll see a face,
or an eye,
10 or the picture ← peculiar images
    of a picture.

Go and open the door.
  If there's a fog ← no image
  it will clear.

Go and open the door.
  Even if there's only
  the darkness ticking, ← ominous image of time passing
  even if there's only
  the hollow wind, ← empty image
20 even if
    nothing ← threatening image
      is there,
go and open the door.

At least
there'll be
a draught. ← unexpected ending

Miroslav Holub

Questions

1 Which idea do you like best?
2 Find two adjectives.
3 a) Which words are repeated?
   b) What effect does this have?
4 What does the poet mean by 'darkness ticking'?

59

Unit 26 : Stop that Monkey Business

Main learning objectives

- To read and evaluate an example of a persuasive letter
- To investigate how style and vocabulary are used to persuade the reader

Whole class

Introduction

This letter was written to a children's magazine from someone who feels strongly about something. While we are reading the letter think about the purpose of the letter – what the writer is trying to do.

Read the letter to the children and discuss it with them. Turn to pages 114–15 for the teacher's version of the text and Questions.

Independent work

Activities: Reading

- Reading Skills A (page 27) or B (page 27).
- To be worked on as an independent exercise.

Guided reading/Extension work

1 Using an enlarged photocopy of the text, underline the words which are used to persuade in one colour, and the words which are used to inform in another colour.

2 Decide which are the most important sentences. If you could have only five sentences which would you select?

3 The editor thought of the headline/title. Why did he choose it? *(It is catchy; a well-known phrase.)* What sort of article would you expect from the headline? Funny? Serious? Jokey? Is it appropriate?

4 Can you think of a better headline/title?

Whole class

Plenary discussion

Discuss how the writer tries to persuade the reader to his point of view. How does he try to make you feel? Which lines are trying to persuade you and which lines are informing you? e.g.'You would have to be a very mean and selfish person. . . creatures' is trying to persuade the reader. 'This charity rescues monkeys' is giving information.

Homework

Write some headlines for a newspaper. You are a journalist and have been investigating cruelty to animals. Use information from the passage, or other examples of cruelty to animals that you know about. Write a selection of headlines. Keep them short and punchy to grab the readers' attention.

Additional activities

Sentence and word work

Re-read the letter and find any useful phrases that could be used to write a persuasive letter on any topic. For instance: 'I am writing to draw your readers' attention', 'I know your readers would want to', 'There have been disgraceful examples of', 'In one appalling instance', 'The problem is', 'However, there are', 'It may be easy to ignore this problem because. . .'

Activities: Writing

- Writing Skills (page 54) – Use the following as the basis for a discussion for and against football in the playground.

  Some reasons for:
  children enjoy it
  it keeps children busy – and out of trouble
  it keeps you healthy (good exercise)
  you can learn ball skills.

  Some reasons against:
  it takes up too much space
  the ball sometimes hits younger children
  the football players don't let other people join in.

- Shared writing (teacher-led) is followed by an independent task.

1. What is the purpose of the letter? *(The children should re-read the first paragraph. The purpose is to draw people's attention to how monkeys are mistreated; to emphasize the need to stop this happening.)*

2. Find two facts used to support the writer's view. *(Re-read the second paragraph – monkeys have been drugged and one was burned with a cigarette.)*

Amusing title – is it appropriate?

UNIT 26

Stop that Monkey Business

persuasive first sentence

introductory paragraph states problem

second paragraph lists facts

★ LETTER OF THE WEEK ★

Dear Sir,

I am writing to draw your readers' attention to a terrible problem. In some countries monkeys are mistreated and mishandled and I know that your readers would want to make sure that such cruelty is stopped.

In Spain, there have been disgraceful examples of monkeys being used by photographers. The monkey sits with tourists whilst their photograph is taken. Tourists may think that this makes a good souvenir. However, what they do not know is that some of the monkeys have been drugged to make sure that they are quiet and sit still. In one appalling instance, a monkey was found covered in cigarette burns. Its owner had burned it to try to keep it under control.

useful word to present case/argument

60

3 Which is the most effective sentence in the last paragraph?*(Various responses – possibly one of the last two sentences.)*

4 Which words, phrases and parts of sentences in the last paragraph are used to persuade the reader. *(Let the children discuss in pairs for a minute or two. Examples are: 'such cruelty exists', 'it may be easy to ignore', 'but I am sure', 'would want to make every effort', 'many adults seem prepared to do nothing', 'you would have to be a very mean and selfish person'.)*

This cruelty happens every day across the world. The problem in Europe is not so bad as it once was. This is mainly thanks to the work of groups based at Monkey World in Dorset. This charity rescues monkeys and keeps them in specially built areas.

However, there are still many other places where such cruelty exists. It may be easy to ignore this problem because we do not see it every day. But I am sure that your readers would want to make every effort to protect monkeys. These animals cannot speak for themselves and many adults seem prepared to do nothing about it. You would have to be a very mean and selfish person not to want to protect harmless creatures.

Yours sincerely

Wayne Perlemann

(Note from the Editor: You can contact Monkey World at the address in the Fact File on the back page of the magazine.)

third paragraph describes positive action

fourth paragraph appeals to readers' better instincts

Monkeys have their own lives and families.

Questions

1 | What is the purpose of the letter?
2 | Find two facts used to support the writer's view.
3 | Which is the most effective sentence in the last paragraph?
4 | Which words, phrases and parts of sentences in the last paragraph are used to persuade the reader?

61

Unit 27 : Bubble and Squeak

Main learning objective

- To identify dilemmas faced by characters and discuss how characters deal with them

Whole class

Introduction

We are going to read an extract from 'The Battle of Bubble and Squeak' by Philippa Pearce. We are going to think about the problem in the story.

When Sid brings two gerbils home, a family battle breaks out. His two sisters, Peggy and Amy, love them, but their mother, Alice, detests them. Their step-dad, Bill, tries to keep the peace. But their mum calls Bubble and Squeak 'smelly rats' and says they must go.

Read the extract to the children and discuss it with them. Turn to pages 118–19 for the teacher's version of the text and Questions.

Independent work

Activities: Reading

- Reading Skills A (page 28) or B (page 28).
- To be worked on as an independent exercise.

Guided reading/Extension work

1 Re-read the second paragraph. Ask the children what they think Mrs Sparrow is feeling while she is kneeling by Amy's bed.
   (She likes the cosiness of cuddling Amy – it is comforting.) Why does she need comforting? Do you think she feels guilty at all about getting cross? Discuss mothers' feelings when they're tired, having to cope with all the children, the mess. Look for clues in the text. *(Sweeping up, checking the children in bed.)*

2 Trace the temperature of Alice Sparrow's feelings: seething like the boiling kettle, then simmering down; then waiting more calmly while the tea brewed – noticing good things about the gerbils; then at the beginning of the fifth paragraph, getting cross again, then thinking about her dead husband, etc. Draw a 'temperature chart' to show her ups and downs.

3 Re-read lines 18–27. What do you think Alice Sparrow would have been like if her husband had been alive and the house swarming with animals?

Whole class

Plenary discussion

Compare notes about the likely outcome. What do you think
Mrs Sparrow feels about her children? Introduce the idea of how
the story might be quite different if she was a cruel mother.

Homework

1 Think of more words and phrases to describe anger, e.g.
seething, boiling, etc. 'like a kettle boiling, like. . .'

2 Think about spellings using silent letters, e.g. 'gnaw'. Find other
words starting with gn, and kn.

Additional activities

Sentence and word work

Look at the use of punctuation in this extract: speech marks,
commas, dashes.

1 There are examples of commas to separate the different parts of
sentences (lines 18–19), and also to separate the items in a
list (lines 23–4), and commas for emphasis – e.g. lines
9–10 and 16. Investigate the use of dashes – showing
that the two things are going on at the same time.
(She sniffs to check that the gerbils don't smell,
interrupting her thought.) Practise reading aloud
lines 8–17, paying attention to the pauses.

2 Study the dialogue on lines 37 and 38, noticing
how the sentences are not complete: 'something
happened?' How do the question marks affect the
way you read it aloud? How do you know it is
Alice speaking in line 38? Turn both phrases into
complete sentences.

Activities: Writing

● Writing Skills (page 56) – writing a letter; persuasive
writing.

● Shared writing (teacher-led) is followed by an
independent task.

Questions

1 Why do you think Mrs Sparrow doesn't want the gerbils? *(Mess, lots of work, she does not like animals.)*

2 What makes her begin to change her mind? *(She relaxes with a cup of tea and notices they are not smelly and do not look like rats.)*

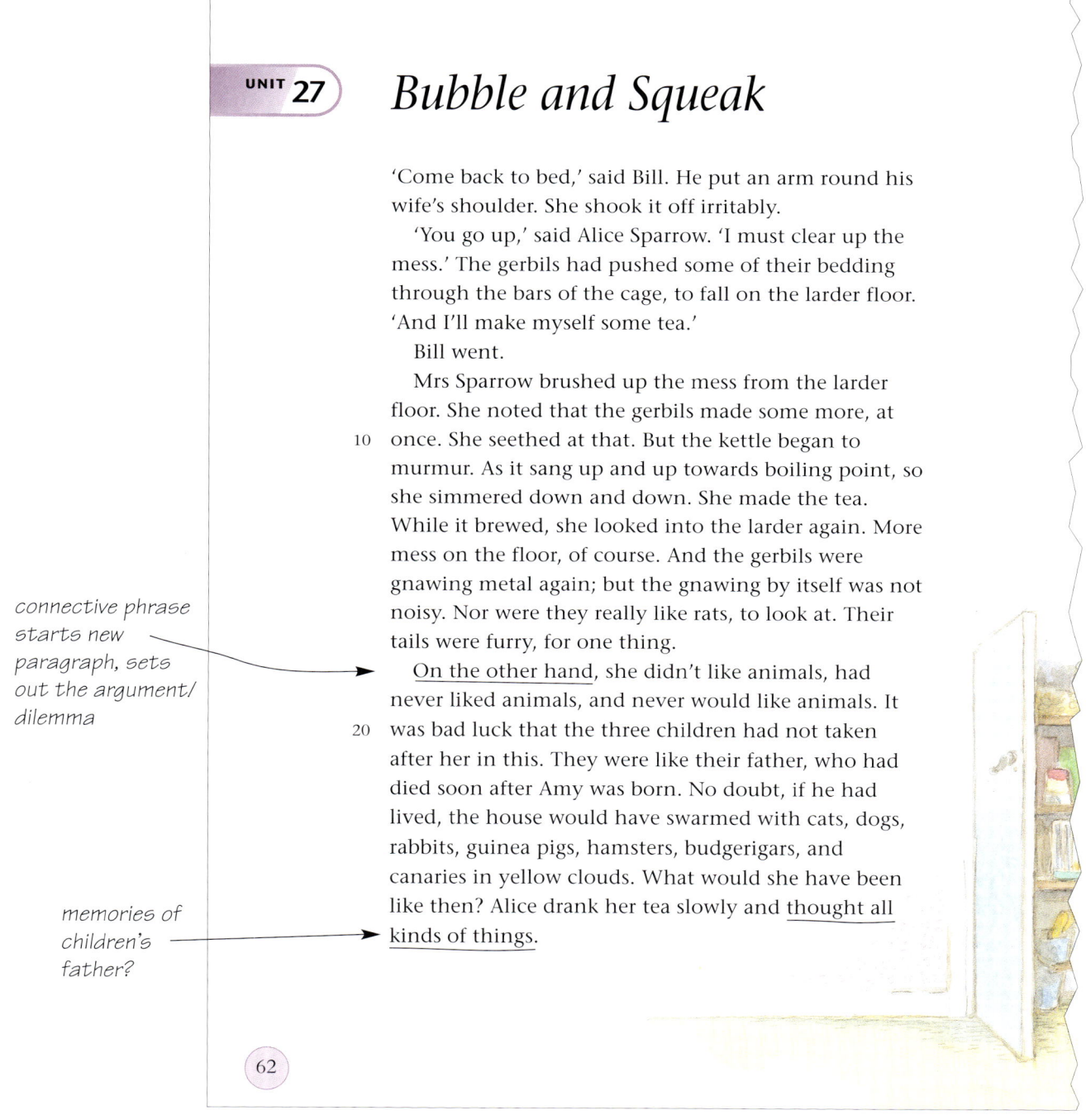

UNIT 27

Bubble and Squeak

'Come back to bed,' said Bill. He put an arm round his wife's shoulder. She shook it off irritably.

'You go up,' said Alice Sparrow. 'I must clear up the mess.' The gerbils had pushed some of their bedding through the bars of the cage, to fall on the larder floor. 'And I'll make myself some tea.'

Bill went.

Mrs Sparrow brushed up the mess from the larder floor. She noted that the gerbils made some more, at once. She seethed at that. But the kettle began to murmur. As it sang up and up towards boiling point, so she simmered down and down. She made the tea. While it brewed, she looked into the larder again. More mess on the floor, of course. And the gerbils were gnawing metal again; but the gnawing by itself was not noisy. Nor were they really like rats, to look at. Their tails were furry, for one thing.

On the other hand, she didn't like animals, had never liked animals, and never would like animals. It was bad luck that the three children had not taken after her in this. They were like their father, who had died soon after Amy was born. No doubt, if he had lived, the house would have swarmed with cats, dogs, rabbits, guinea pigs, hamsters, budgerigars, and canaries in yellow clouds. What would she have been like then? Alice drank her tea slowly and thought all kinds of things.

connective phrase starts new paragraph, sets out the argument/ dilemma

memories of children's father?

62

3 Why do you think Sid's shoulder is 'hunched high like a wall'? *(He is upset and angry with his mum.)*

4 What might she be thinking as she cuddles Amy? *(Remembering the children's father who loved animals, thinking about the old days and how much she loves her children, trying to decide what to do.)*

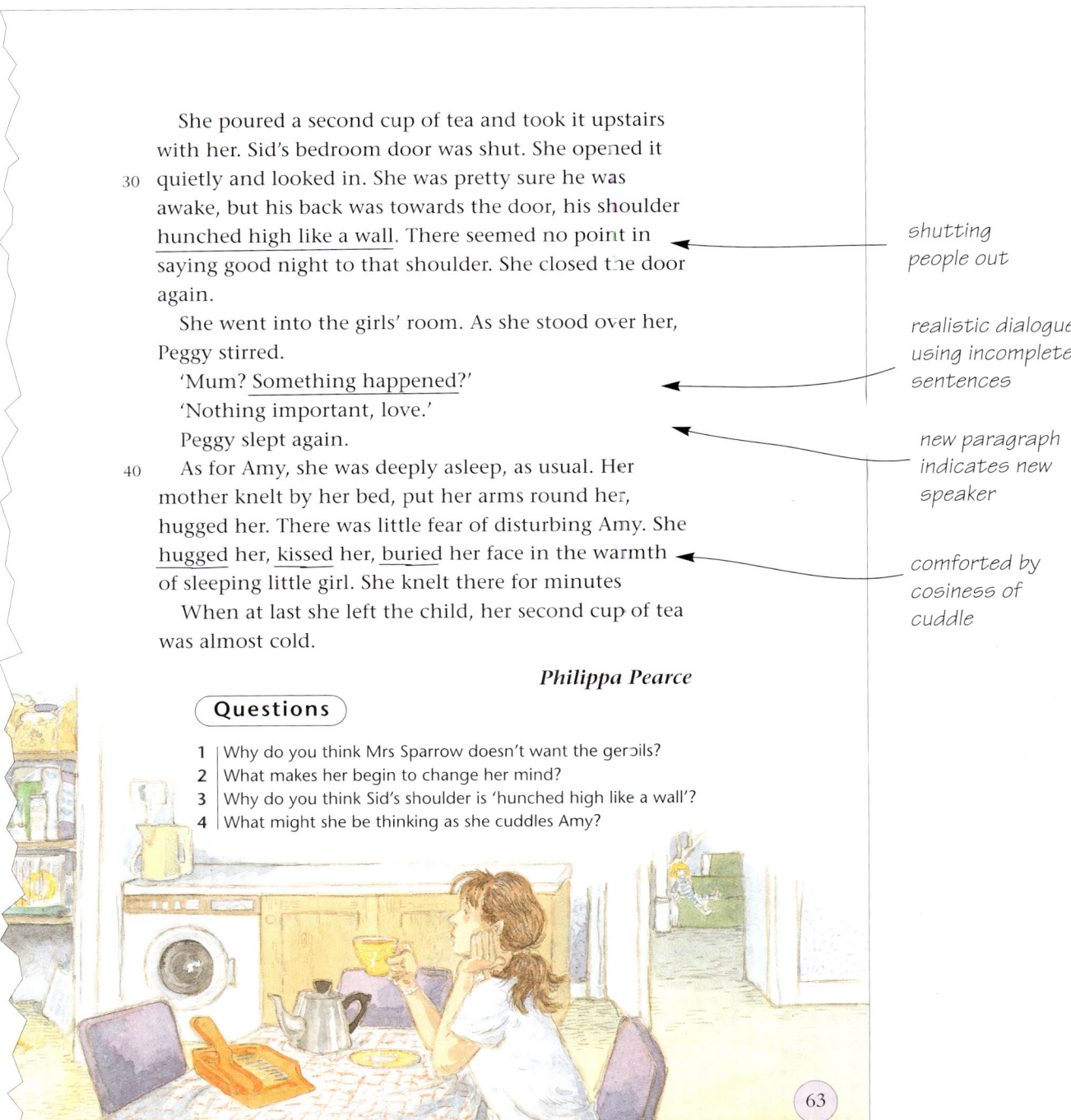

She poured a second cup of tea and took it upstairs with her. Sid's bedroom door was shut. She opened it
30 quietly and looked in. She was pretty sure he was awake, but his back was towards the door, his shoulder hunched high like a wall. There seemed no point in saying good night to that shoulder. She closed the door again.

She went into the girls' room. As she stood over her, Peggy stirred.

'Mum? Something happened?'

'Nothing important, love.'

Peggy slept again.

40 As for Amy, she was deeply asleep, as usual. Her mother knelt by her bed, put her arms round her, hugged her. There was little fear of disturbing Amy. She hugged her, kissed her, buried her face in the warmth of sleeping little girl. She knelt there for minutes

When at last she left the child, her second cup of tea was almost cold.

Philippa Pearce

— shutting people out

— realistic dialogue using incomplete sentences

— new paragraph indicates new speaker

— comforted by cosiness of cuddle

Questions

1 | Why do you think Mrs Sparrow doesn't want the gerbils?
2 | What makes her begin to change her mind?
3 | Why do you think Sid's shoulder is 'hunched high like a wall'?
4 | What might she be thinking as she cuddles Amy?

63

Unit 28 : Homework – Should it be Compulsory?

Main learning objectives

- To investigate how arguments are structured and presented
- To investigate how style and vocabulary are used to persuade the reader

Whole class

Introduction

This piece of writing sets out an argument to persuade the reader about an important issue for many children. The government has been considering making it compulsory for every child to do half an hour of homework every night. While we read through the passage think about what the writer's opinion is and how they organize their writing.

Read the extract to the children and discuss it with them. Make sure the children understand the word 'compulsory'. Turn to page 122 for the teacher's version of the text and Questions.

Independent work

Activities: Reading

- Reading Skills A (page 29) or B (page 29).
- To be worked on in pairs.

Guided reading/Extension work

1 List further reasons for or against having compulsory homework.
2 Experiment with different sentences by changing them from statements into questions. Write questions and their answers using information from the passage.
3 Discuss how changing the type of sentence alters word order and punctuation.

Whole class

Plenary discussion

1 Discuss whether the writer presents a fair argument. Consider how they present a balanced view by giving a similar number of reasons for and against, with examples/evidence. Only at the end does the writer apparently decide.
2 Re-read the second and third paragraphs. Discuss the difference between the arguments and the supporting examples.

Homework

Use **Worksheet 33** (Homework Interview). Interview people at home to find out what they think about homework. Use the Worksheet to record the interview information. Be ready to give feedback to the class the following day.

Additional activities

Sentence and word work

1 Read through the passage and find key phrases that could be used in any argument, in a logical order, e.g.

   a) . . . have been discussing whether or not. . .

   b) The main reasons for supporting this idea are. . .
       For instance. . .
       Another good reason is. . .

   c) The main argument against this idea is that. . .
       For instance. . .
       Also. . .

   d) However, even though there are good reasons against. . .
       I believe that. . .
       In addition. . .

   Add these to the wall chart framework you made under Questions. List each phrase under the most appropriate heading.

Activities: Writing

- Writing Skills (page 58) – making notes on the passage.
- Shared writing (teacher-led) is followed by an independent task.

1. What is the viewpoint of the writer? *(Ask the children where they should look to find the writer's conclusion – that homework is a good idea. Re-read the final paragraph.)*

2. What does each paragraph tell you? Give it a heading. *(1. What you are discussing. 2. The reasons for – with some evidence ('for instance').*

3. *Reasons against with some evidence ('for instance'). 4. What the writer decides, with reasons.)*

3. How could you use this information as a framework for writing a different argument? *(Write the headings up as a wall chart. Explain that it can be used as a planning sheet and to help the children to plan their writing.)*

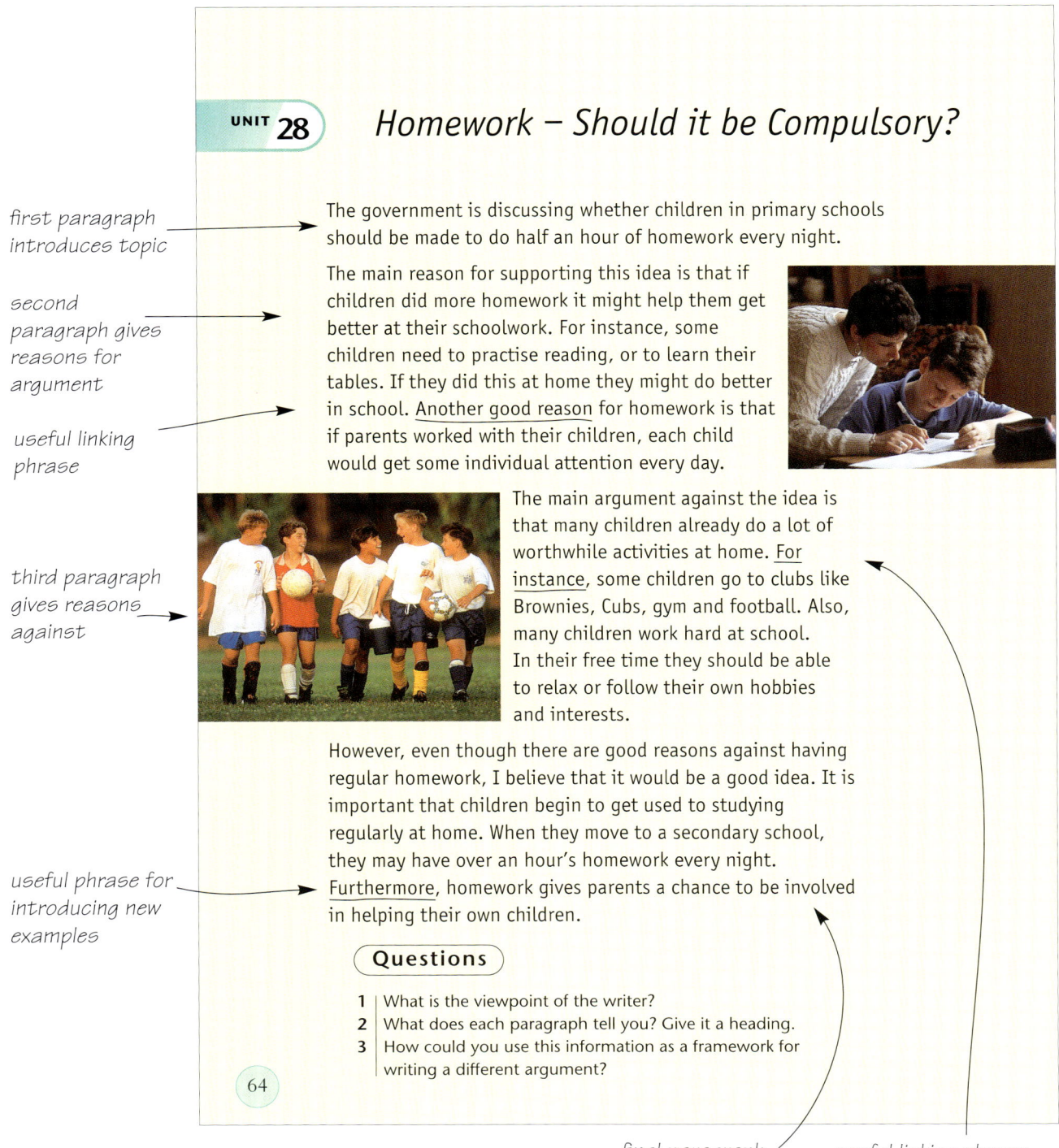

UNIT **28**

Homework – Should it be Compulsory?

first paragraph introduces topic

The government is discussing whether children in primary schools should be made to do half an hour of homework every night.

second paragraph gives reasons for argument

The main reason for supporting this idea is that if children did more homework it might help them get better at their schoolwork. For instance, some children need to practise reading, or to learn their tables. If they did this at home they might do better in school. <u>Another good reason</u> for homework is that if parents worked with their children, each child would get some individual attention every day.

useful linking phrase

third paragraph gives reasons against

The main argument against the idea is that many children already do a lot of worthwhile activities at home. <u>For instance</u>, some children go to clubs like Brownies, Cubs, gym and football. Also, many children work hard at school. In their free time they should be able to relax or follow their own hobbies and interests.

However, even though there are good reasons against having regular homework, I believe that it would be a good idea. It is important that children begin to get used to studying regularly at home. When they move to a secondary school, they may have over an hour's homework every night. <u>Furthermore</u>, homework gives parents a chance to be involved in helping their own children.

useful phrase for introducing new examples

Questions

1. What is the viewpoint of the writer?
2. What does each paragraph tell you? Give it a heading.
3. How could you use this information as a framework for writing a different argument?

64

final paragraph draws conclusion   *useful linking phrase*

Glossary

abbreviation   a word which is shortened, e.g., 'Mr' (mister).

adjective   a word or phrase which is added to a noun to describe it. It may come before or after the noun, e.g., The *tall* man; the man *was tall*.

adverb   a word or phrase which describes a verb. Many adverbs can be made by adding the suffix '-ly' to an adjective, e.g., 'slow-ly'.

alliteration   a phrase where words which are adjacent or close begin with the same phoneme, e.g.,'beautiful, big bubbles'; 'knowing neighbours'.

apostrophe (')   a punctuation mark indicating contraction (*don't* for *do not*) or possession (the *boy's* book).

blurb   information about a book, usually printed on the book cover.

calligram   a poem in which the way the letters are formed (or the type face chosen) reflects the theme, e.g., a poem about anger written in spiky letters.

clause   *main clause* – the main part of the sentence which makes sense on its own, e.g., *We are going out* when he gets back.
subordinate clause – group of words from a sentence which do not make sense alone, e.g., We are going out *when he gets back*.

climax   the highest or most exciting point (e.g., of a film or a story).

collective noun   names a group of people or things, e.g., crowd, team, herd.

colon (:)   a punctuation mark often used to introduce a list or a quotation.

comma (,)   a punctuation mark indicating a pause between parts of a sentence.

conflict   a struggle; in a story, the part where things go wrong or two or more forces are opposed.

connective   words and phrases used to link different parts of a text (clauses, sentences, paragraphs or chapters): and, because, unless, finally, suddenly, etc.

construction   the way a thing is put together; in a sentence, the arrangement of the words and phrases.

contraction   words which are shortened or which comprise two words shortened into one, e.g., can't = can not.

crisis   a crucial time, a turning point in events – usually when things are at their worst.

derivation   the origin of a word or saying.

dialogue   a conversation between two people.

discussion text   a text which presents all sides of an issue.

draft   preliminary version of a text; writing often goes through several drafts before the finished version.

edit   to correct or alter written work before publication. This takes place after drafting and revising and before proof-reading (a final check for errors).

exclamation mark   punctuation mark used at the end of a sentence to indicate strong feeling.

explanation text   text which explains a process.

fairy tale   a story written for, or told to, children which includes magic.

fiction   a story invented by the writer with imaginary settings, characters and events.

fable   a short story with a moral lesson. Animals are often used as characters.

first person (written in the)   written from the point of view of the person speaking, e.g., *I* left home.

fonts   typefaces.

genre   a term referring to different types of writing, e.g., *ghost story, letter, sonnet*.

glossary   an alphabetical list explaining the unfamiliar words used in a book.

grammar   the rules and conventions which govern the way language is used.

guided reading   pupils are taught in groups according to reading ability. The teacher works with each group on a shared text at an appropriate level of challenge.

guided writing   pupils are grouped by writing ability. The teacher works with each group at an appropriate level of challenge.

haiku   a poem (after the Japanese model) with three lines and 17 syllables, in the pattern 5,7,5.

half-rhyme   words which almost rhyme, e.g., *leaf/loaf; peat/bean*.

homonym   a word with the same spelling as another but with a different meaning.

homophone   words which sound the same but which have a different meaning, e.g., *bear/bare*.

hyphen   a punctuation mark which joins two words or parts of words together, e.g., non-fiction, re-read.

imagery   use of language to create a vivid sensory picture – painting with words; includes use of similes and metaphors.

informal   in writing – use of language which may not follow all the usual conventions, using unconventional grammar, contractions, slang, etc; especially, using some of the conventions of speech.

kenning   a phrase (from Old Norse poetry) which describes something without using its name, e.g., *sweet-smeller, finger-pricker, summer-bloomer* (to describe a rose).

key word   a word which is important in giving the reader a clue to the meaning of a piece of text.

layout   arrangement of material (text and illustrations) on a page.

legend   traditional story about heroic characters such as King Arthur, perhaps originally based on truth.

limerick   a comic verse with 5 lines following the syllable pattern 8,8,6,6,8 and the rhyme scheme AABBA.

metaphor   when the writer says that one thing is another, e.g., *the sea is a hungry dog* also, to suggest that one thing is something else, e.g., *the telegraph poles stood to attention* (suggesting they are soldiers).

mood   the 'feel' or atmosphere of a text.

moral   a lesson taught by an example, e.g., in a fable or story.

myth   a story about gods or heroes – usually explaining some fact in nature, e.g., why the sun rises every morning.

narrative poem   a poem which tells a story.

noun   name of a person, place, object or feature.

onomatopoeia   words whose sound reflects their meaning, e.g., *hiss, buzz*.

pen portrait   a written, usually brief, description of someone.

person   *first* person (*I* went).
second person (*you* went).
third person (*she* went).

phoneme   the smallest unit of sound in a word. There are about 44 phonemes in English. A phoneme may be represented by one, two, three or four letters, e.g., *go, mow, though*.

phrase   a group of words which form a unit but not a sentence.

> *noun phrase* – the house, their red shoes.
> *verb phrase* – we *skipped along.*
> *adverbial phrase* – answers the questions how? when? or where? about the verb, e.g., we drove *under the bridge.*
> *adjectival phrase* – a phrase used as an adjective, e.g., The old man *with the grey beard.*
> *prepositional phrase* – explains how two nouns are related, beginning with a preposition, e.g., The car is *under the bridge.*

predict   say what is going to happen in the part of a text not yet read.

prefix   form which can be added to the beginning of a word, to change its meaning, e.g., *un*happy; *in*decisive.

preposition   words which describe position or the relationship between two words (*after, for, with*). Words like *in, over, under,* are prepositions.

pronoun   a word used instead of the noun which comes before it, e.g., The cat is asleep. *She* is on the sofa.

proof-read   to check a piece of work throughly before publication.

punctuation   a way of marking written text to help the reader to understand. For example full stop, comma, apostrophe.

question mark   punctuation mark used at the end of a sentence to indicate a question.

rap   oral poetry with a very strong rhythm and fast pace, originally from the Caribbean and Afro-Caribbean cultures.

recount text   a text written to retell for information or entertainment.

report   a text written to describe or give information, e.g., about dinosaurs.

resolution   the part of a story where problems are sorted out so that the story can reach a satisfactory conclusion.

rhyme   words containing the same rhyme in their final syllable.

rhyming couplet   two lines which rhyme in their final syllable.

role play   acting the part of someone else, e.g., a character in a book.

scan   move quickly through a text looking for the answers to specific questions; stopping when you spot key words and phrases (words which relate to the question).

screenplay   detailed script of a film usually including technical directions such as camera position.

scribe   to write on behalf of others, e.g., teacher writing down the words dictated by children.

semi colon (;)   a punctuation mark used to separate phrases or clauses in a sentence; stronger than a comma but less strong than a full stop.

sentence   a unit of language which makes sense on its own; beginning with a capital letter, ending with a full stop, question mark or exclamation mark.

> *simple sentence* – with only one clause: e.g., 'I went to the doctor.'
> *compound/complex sentence* – made up of simple sentences joined by conjunctions: 'I went to the doctor because my leg hurt.'

shared writing   the teacher models the writing process. Children can be involved in planning, composition, editing and publishing.

simile   when one thing is compared to another using the words 'like' or 'as', e.g., 'An old leaf is *like a map*' or 'Dad's temper is *as sharp as a smack*'.

skim   move quickly through a text to get a general idea of what it is about – quickly focusing on headings and sub-headings to gain an impression of content.

slang   popular, very informal words and phrases.

speech   *direct:* the words actually spoken, indicated by speech marks, e.g., 'Go away!' he shouted.
> *indirect/reported:* the words are reported but not quoted, without speech marks, e.g. He told me to go away.

statement   something expressed clearly in words.

story board   a visual plan for a story (video, film, book, etc) which shows the plot and main events through a series of pictures.

story stages   the sections of a story which give it its shape – e.g., *beginning/middle/end* or *build-up/ conflict/climax/resolution.*

structure   the shape of a text; the way it is put together to give it shape.

style   the way a writer achieves effects; slightly different in every writer, for instance; using a lot of dialogue; very informal language; a lot of short sentences.

suffix   form which can be added to the end of a word, to change its meaning: e.g., eat*ing*; lean*ed*; sing*er*; ghost*ly*.

syllable pattern   the pattern made by adding up the number of syllables in each line. For example, a haiku has three lines whose syllable pattern is 5,7,5.

synonym   word which has the same or similar meaning to another, e.g., *old/aged; said/called.*

tense   indicates *when* something is happening:
> *past:* He ate.
> *present:* He eats.
> *future:* He will eat.
> *continuous:* He is eating.

thesaurus   a reference text which groups words by meaning. Can help writers to choose alternative words.

verb   word or group of words which names an action or state of being (being or doing words). Verbs may be in different tenses.
> *past:* I saw, I have seen.
> *present:* I see, I am seeing, I do see.
> *future:* I will see, I will be seeing.

viewpoint   point of view – through whose eyes something is seen.

vowel   a, e, i, o, u; every syllable contains a vowel.

writing frame   a structure or template for a piece of writing; often including opening phrases.